A History of the Battle of Britain Fighter Association

A History of the Battle of Britain Fighter Association

Commemorating the Few

Geoff Simpson

Pen & Sword
AVIATION

First published in Great Britain in 2015 by
Pen & Sword Aviation
an imprint of
Pen & Sword Books Ltd
47 Church Street
Barnsley
South Yorkshire
S70 2AS

ISBN 978 1 78159 387 5

A CIP catalogue record for this book is available from the British
Library

Typeset in Ehrhardt by
Mac Style Ltd, Bridlington, East Yorkshire
Printed and bound in the UK by CPI Group (UK) Ltd,
Croydon, CRO 4YY

Pen & Sword Books Ltd incorporates the imprints of Pen & Sword
Archaeology, Atlas, Aviation, Battleground, Discovery, Family History,
History, Maritime, Military, Naval, Politics, Railways, Select, Transport,
True Crime, and Fiction, Frontline Books, Leo Cooper, Praetorian
Press, Seaforth Publishing and Wharncliffe.

For a complete list of Pen & Sword titles please contact
PEN & SWORD BOOKS LIMITED
47 Church Street, Barnsley, South Yorkshire, S70 2AS, England
E-mail: enquiries@pen-and-sword.co.uk
Website: www.pen-and-sword.co.uk

Contents

'Of all the British combatants of the Second World War, the 'few' have attained a unique and legendary place in the historiography of the war.'
Dr Jeremy A. Crang, writing in *War & Society*, November 2005

'The object of giving medals, stars and ribbons is to give pride and pleasure to those who have deserved them. At the same time a distinction is something which everybody does not possess. If all have it, it is of less value. There must, therefore, be heartburnings and disappointments on the border line. A medal glitters, but it also casts a shadow. The task of drawing up regulations for such awards is one which does not admit of a perfect solution. It is not possible to satisfy everybody without running the risk of satisfying nobody. All that is possible is to give the greatest satisfaction to the greatest number and to hurt the feelings of the fewest. But that is a most difficult task and it is easy to err on one side or the other. One must be careful in the first place to avoid profusion. The tendency to expand, shall I say inflate, dilute the currency through generous motives, is very strong.'
Winston Churchill, as Prime Minister, addressing the House of Commons, 22 March 1944

Foreword by HRH The Prince of Wales

CLARENCE HOUSE

As Patron of the Battle of Britain Fighter Association, I am delighted that a history of this most exclusive, revered and admired club has been written to commemorate seventy-five years since the Summer of 1940. Having taken on the Patronage of the Association from my beloved Grandmother in 2003, I have attended many of the services and reunions organized by the Association and have greatly enjoyed getting to know such a remarkable group of men.

As a child, I well remember the stories told by my Grandmother and Mother about the Battle of Britain. Their vivid descriptions of dogfights over Southern England and bombing raids on Buckingham Palace, as aircrew defended this nation from Nazi invasion, have stayed with me ever since. In company with many others, these stories of heroism, tenacity and skill – against overwhelming odds – have helped to imbue a deep respect and admiration for all those who flew at this pivotal time in the last war. At a young age, I had the privilege of meeting some of the pilots who served in the Battle, including Douglas Bader, and was struck by their modesty and sense of camaraderie. This sense of camaraderie remains with "the Few" today, helped so magnificently by the work of the Association.

Of course, many aircrew tragically paid the ultimate price in defence of this country, with others enduring lives blighted by horrific injuries. However, if they had failed in their endeavour, the consequences for this island and the world would have been unimaginable.

The Battle of Britain Fighter Association, founded in 1958, has undertaken sterling work supporting veterans of the Battle of Britain, and keeping "the Few", drawn from fourteen nations, in the public eye. As an exceptionally proud Patron of the Association, I am so pleased that a history of its work has been written, reflecting the courage and fortitude of those who served in the Battle of Britain. Seventy-five years on, we still owe them an immense and irredeemable debt of gratitude.

A Message from the Chairman of the Battle of Britain Fighter Association

Over many years the Battle of Britain Fighter Association has brought together those who flew in Fighter Command in the summer and autumn of 1940. The camaraderie which we have always enjoyed continues. Now our key task is to ensure that what was achieved 75 years ago by so many men and women in all three services, as well as civilians, is remembered long into the future.

Commemoration of those deeds began in the early years of the war and has continued ever since.

From that time there was also much discussion on whether Allied airmen who took part in the battle should be given a symbol to wear and, if so, what form it should take. Alongside that discussion was one about who should be entitled to wear such a symbol. The announcement of the Battle of Britain Clasp to the 1939–1945 Star was made in 1945, yet even to this day the research continues into some 'doubtful cases' amongst Fighter Command airmen who were or were not awarded the clasp.

I am, therefore, delighted that Geoff Simpson has made a new contribution to Battle of Britain literature by exploring the history of the Fighter Association, alongside a consideration of the award of the clasp and the commemoration of the battle.

Wing Commander Bob Foster DFC AE
Chairman Battle of Britain Fighter Association

Sadly Bob Foster died on 30 July 2014. His widow Kaethe has asked that his message should still appear.

A Message from the Chief of the Air Staff

The Battle of Britain is recognised as both a key moment in British history and one of the proudest episodes in the history of the Royal Air Force. It was a time when all the home commands of the Service played their part in ensuring that this country did not suffer foreign invasion.

Three quarters of a century after this great event it is right that a record should be made of the way in which it is commemorated. I believe that it is essential too that future generations continue to remember the Battle of Britain.

Air Chief Marshal Sir Andrew Pulford KCB CBE ADC
Chief of the Air Staff

Introduction

The Battle of Britain has become one of the most famous, celebrated, recorded and analysed events in British history. There is so much we know about the events of 1940, a year which was certainly a fulcrum in that history, yet there is also much still to be learned.

Though the official definition of the battle was not established until after the war in Europe had ended, commemoration of what was seen as a victory by the Royal Air Force had begun well before that. The desire to establish the names of the men who had flown on the British side in the battle was established very early and so was the concept of an emblem for the participants to wear.

Those participants were rarely conscious at the time that they were fighting something called 'The Battle of Britain' and they certainly did not realise on 10 July or 31 October 1940 that a significant moment was passing. Such is the nature of arbitrary definitions.

Members of 'The Few', as Winston Churchill had caused them to be named, met in comradeship after the war. Eventually, in 1958, they formally came together and established the Battle of Britain Fighter Association. There was then a gap of thirty-five years, remarkable as it may seem now, before a National Memorial to The Few was established at Capel-le-Ferne on the Kentish cliffs outside Folkestone.

Celebrity came suddenly to the men of Fighter Command. At the time of the evacuation from the Channel ports in the spring of 1940, the RAF was accused of doing too little to help the Army. The charge was without foundation, but it was believed by many of those on the beaches and harbour-sides waiting for rescue and by many waiting at home in fear of invasion.

With the 'miracle of Dunkirk' achieved, the aerial fighting developed over the English Channel, then moved inland. Now the people of south-east England in particular could see Fighter Command in action and bear witness to the heroism that was being displayed. Now stories began to abound of women kissing airmen in the street, drinks being bought for them and taxi drivers refusing to accept their money.

The contrast was a stark one so there is sometimes some cynicism in the attitude of 'The Few' to their fame. It manifests itself not least when they make the standard reply to questions about how they felt on 20 August 1940 when the Prime Minister made the speech that created 'The Few'. Ask them how they felt then and they very often think back to: 'Never in the field of human conflict was so much owed by so many to so few,' and make the response: 'Oh, we thought he was talking about our mess bills'.

For the rest of their lives the survivors were marked out by their service over less than four months in the first full year of the war. No doubt that has often been a source of pleasure to them, though the attention can also be irksome. Brian Kingcome, a Spitfire pilot in the battle, apparently remarked that if the fuss continued he would take to wearing his medals on his pyjamas.

Over many years it has been an enormous privilege to come to know many of the men who flew in the Battle of Britain. To be given the full co-operation of the Battle of Britain Fighter Association in the writing of this book, including access to its archives, was a much appreciated and added honour.

Geoff Simpson
21 August 2014

Abbreviations

AE	Air Efficiency Award
AFC	Air Force Cross
AHB	Air Historical Branch (RAF)
AMO	Air Ministry Order
BBFA	Battle of Britain Fighter Association
CB	Companion of the Order of the Bath
Cpl	Corporal
CWGC	Commonwealth War Graves Commission
DFC	Distinguished Flying Cross
DFM	Distinguished Flying Medal
Dr	Doctor
DSO	Distinguished Service Order
Fg Off	Flying Officer
Flt Lt	Flight Lieutenant
HMSO	His/Her Majesty's Stationery Office
HQ	Headquarters
IWGC	Imperial War Graves Commission
IWM	Imperial War Museum
KCB	Knight Commander of the Bath
KCVO	Knight Commander of the Royal Victorian Order
MBE	Member of the Order of the British Empire
MC	Military Cross
MP	Member of Parliament
NCO	Non-Commissioned Officer
OBE	Officer of the Order of the British Empire
OC	Officer Commanding
OM	Order of Merit
ORB	Operations Record Book
PM	Prime Minister

PoW   Prisoner of War
RAF   Royal Air Force
RAFA   Royal Air Forces Association
RAFO   Reserve of Air Force Officers
RAAF   Royal Australian Air Force
RAuxAF   Royal Auxiliary Air Force
RAFVR   Royal Air Force Volunteer Reserve
RDF   Radio Direction Finding (Radar)
Rev   Reverend
RNAS   Royal Naval Air Station
RNVR   Royal Naval Volunteer Reserve
ROC   Royal Observer Corps
Sqn Ldr   Squadron Leader
VC   Victoria Cross
Wg Cdr   Wing Commander

Acknowledgements

Many people, including The Few themselves, have helped me over the years to try to understand the matters dealt with in this book. All too often and very sadly, those mentioned here are no longer with us.

I give especial thanks to:

Group Captain Patrick Tootal OBE DL, the Secretary of the Battle of Britain Fighter Association and his immediate predecessors, Malcolm Smith MBE and Wing Commander Pat Hancock OBE DFC. Patrick Tootal gave me full access to the archives of the BBFA.

Wing Commander Bob Foster DFC AE, Chairman of the BBFA until his death in 2014, was a source of much advice and information, as were the two Chairmen before him, Air Commodore 'Pete' Brothers CBE DSO DFC and bar and Air Chief Marshal Sir Christopher Foxley-Norris GCB DSO OBE.

Wing Commander John Young AFC and Group Captain Tom Gleave CBE, were archivists of the BBFA who were, without fail, willing to share their knowledge. Much of the paperwork that they accumulated is now held at the Air Historical Branch (RAF) at Northolt.

Amongst the men entitled to wear the Battle of Britain Clasp, particular insights on the BBFA, the clasp and the commemoration of the battle came from (apart from those already mentioned): Squadron Leader Cyril Bamberger DFC and bar AE, Wing Commander John Beazley DFC, Flight Lieutenant Owen Burns, Flying Officer Ron Forward, Squadron Leader Tony Pickering AE, Flight Lieutenant William Walker AE and Flying Officer Ken Wilkinson.

My fellow Trustees, as well as Life Vice Presidents, of the Battle of Britain Memorial Trust, have always been helpful and encouraging in my research, including the founder of the Trust, Wing Commander Geoffrey Page DSO OBE DFC and bar, Air Chief Marshal Sir Michael Graydon GCB, CBE, the current President, Richard Hunting CBE, the Chairman, Air Chief Marshal

Sir Peter Squire GCB DFC AFC, Group Captain John Hollowood, Wing Commander Andy Simpson and Colin Smith.

Sebastian Cox, Head of the Air Historical Branch (RAF) provided me with facilities and gave me the enormous benefit of his advice. His colleague Neil Chamberlain was also most helpful.

Dr Jeremy Crang of the University of Edinburgh was, as always, most generous in allowing me to use the results of his research, not least as recorded in *War & Society*.

Edward McManus and Gerry Burke willingly shared their vast knowledge acquired in the search for the stories of The Few.

Victoria Thompson cheerfully allowed herself to be persuaded to help with research and yet again found outstanding material.

Kristen Alexander's passionate and erudite research into the Australian Clasp holders and their commemoration has added greatly to my knowledge of the subject.

Bernadette Archer, Librarian, Word & Image Department, Victoria and Albert Museum
Colonel Pierre-Alain Antoine
Colonel Paul Beaver
Peter Bebbington
Marie Blake
D.L. Bradley
David Brocklehurst MBE, Kent Battle of Britain Museum
Nancy, Anthony and Caroline Case
Jeff Cherrington, National Trust
Laurie Chester, Custodian, St George's Royal Air Force Chapel of Remembrance, Biggin Hill
John Clarke
Rita and Andrew Clarke, Headcorn Branch, Royal Air Forces Association
Peter Collins, Rolls-Royce Heritage Trust
Bob Cossey, 74 Squadron Association
Hazel Crozier, Curator, RAF College, Cranwell
Philip Curtis
Claire Darke, Secretary, Wolverhampton Civic and Historical Society
Professor Gerard De Groot
Nigel Denchfield

Tom Dolezal
Josefina de Vasconcellos
Group Captain Alex Dickson OBE QVRM AE
Fred Dunster
Wing Commander Erica Ferguson, Bentley Priory Battle of Britain Trust
Barry Fletcher
Sharman and John Flindall
'Bunny' Ford
Gary Godel
Roy Goodey, London at War Study Group
Dr Adrian Gregory
John Hall
Mary Hancock
Mark Hillier
Margaret Hobbs, Brookwood Cemetery Society
Christopher Jeens, Archivist, Gloucester Cathedral Library
Melissa John
Bob Kingaby
Peter Knottley
Michael Korda
Adrienne and Philippe Lecoeuvre
Lois MacDonell
Martin Mace
Sean Maffett
Dr Tony Mansell
Barry M. Marsden
Clive Millman
Stuart Millson
Bernie Morel
Geneviève Moulard
Simon Muggleton
National Maritime Museum
The 2nd Lord Newall DL
Tim Pierce, College Hall Library, RAF College, Cranwell
Jacquie Pinney, Chief Executive, Blond McIndoe Research Foundation
Air Commodore Graham Pitchfork MBE
Fergus Read, Imperial War Museums

Ian Quickfall, Archivist, Malvern College
Christine Reynolds, Assistant Keeper of the Muniments, Westminster Abbey
St Laurence's Church, Ludlow
Salesian College, Farnborough, Hampshire
Andy Saunders
Julian Shaw
Mark Sheridan
Margaret Simpson
Marigold Simpson
Joyce Smith
Shirley Starkey
Marshal of the Royal Air Force The Lord Stirrup KG GCB AFC
The 3rd Viscount Thurso
Janet Tootal BEM
Anthony Tuck
Peter Vincent
Dr Brian Woods-Scawen CBE DL
Kenneth G. Wynn
Wing Commander Mike Yule

Chapter One

Definition Of The Battle

As explained in detail in this book, to qualify for the 'immediate' award of the 1939–1945 Star with Battle of Britain Clasp, an airman had to make one operational flight with one of seventy-one squadrons and other units under the control of RAF Fighter Command between 10 July 1940 and 31 October 1940.

The Battle Of Britain

After months of so called 'Phoney War' since 3 September 1939, German forces began an assault on France and the Low Countries on 10 May 1940. On the same day, though it was not cause and effect, Winston Churchill succeeded Neville Chamberlain as British Prime Minister.

The British Expeditionary Force in France and Belgium was soon forced to retreat in the face of the German Blitzkrieg. The evacuation of British and Allied troops took place from Dunkirk and other Channel ports.

On 18 June 1940 Churchill made the speech in the House of Commons, which is often remembered for his call to, *'so bear ourselves that, if the British Empire and its Commonwealth last for a thousand years, men will still say: "This was their finest hour"'*.

Earlier in the speech he had said:

> *'What General Weygand called the Battle of France is over. I expect that the Battle of Britain is about to begin.'*

Weygand was the veteran French General appointed Allied Commander in Chief on 17 May. Churchill's summation of what was to come would shortly enter the language. He repeated his speech 'almost word for word' according to his private secretary, 'Jock' Colville, on the radio that evening.

Churchill's speech also set out to reassure the public that much military might remained in the United Kingdom. It is clear that Hitler was determined to take Britain out of the war and The Battle of Britain was fought to achieve German air superiority as a prelude to invasion.

Most historians agree that the Battle of Britain can be divided into a number of phases, though there is not always agreement on the dates of those phases. Typically it might be argued that the divisions were:

- 10 July–7 August – fighting over the sea
- 8–23 August – Lead up to Adler Tag (Eagle Day), the day itself and its aftermath
- 24 August–6 September – Attacks on airfields, chain home stations and aircraft factories
- 7–30 September – The emphasis of the attacks switches further inland, notably including London
- 1 October–31 October – The battle quietens. Attacks at night and high level sorties which attempt to take Fighter Command aircraft beyond acceptable operational ceilings.

It is sometimes claimed, with some justification, that 8 August was actually the last day of the first phase, as its main feature was the fighting over a convoy known as CW9 to the Royal Navy and 'Peewit' to the RAF, as it made its way westwards along the English Channel.

A good many precise figures are quoted as to the exact number of Allied airmen who took part in the Battle of Britain, most of them between 2,917 and 2,980. In fact, nobody knows for sure, although a reasonable estimate would be around 2,940.

There are a number of reasons for the doubt. They include the fact that the official definition of the battle changed somewhat, so that there were people who at one stage qualified for the clasp and then lost that status. There seems to have been some over-generous issuing of clasps. There were those who qualified but did not wish to be considered as Battle of Britain participants, perhaps because they had seen no action or enemy aircraft at that time. Inevitably there have been those who muddied the waters by claiming entitlement to the clasp without justification, perhaps even wearing it on military occasions. It is understandable that the degree of attention given to keeping squadron records was not always assiduous in the circumstances of 1940 and some records were destroyed.

In addition, the research goes on. There are those who appear on credible lists of The Few whose entitlement might be debatable (rather than clearly non-existent) and there are probably a very few men still to be identified.

The creation of the concept of 'The Few'
When the Prime Minister, Winston Churchill, rose to make a speech to the House of Commons on 20 August 1940 the time was recorded as 3.52pm by Hansard. Mr Churchill began by remarking that, *Almost a year has passed since the war began, and it is natural, I think, to pause on our journey at this milestone and survey the dark, wide field.'*

'Jock' Colville, one of the Prime Minister's private secretaries, noted in his diary that many hours had been spent preparing the speech and that, as was the Churchillian habit, key phrases in it had been chewed over time and again. The lines that were later to become world-renowned had certainly been uttered on one previous occasion, or at least a version of them had. That was four days previously as the Prime Minister left the No 11 Group operations room at Uxbridge.

According to Colville the Commons speech, apart from some bright patches, seemed to drag and the House was 'languid'. Most interest was aroused by the account given of the deal with the United States whereby the Americans would operate from air bases in the West Indies. So, on the evidence of one witness, there was no sense at the time that the speech being delivered contained a passage that would be constantly quoted down the years as a great historical statement.

The Prime Minister had remarked that, *'The great air battle which has been in progress over this Island for the last few weeks has recently attained a high intensity. It is too soon to attempt to assign limits either to its scale or to its duration.'*

A couple of minutes later, after praising the work of the Ministry of Aircraft Production, he told the House:

> *'The gratitude of every home in our Island, in our Empire, and indeed throughout the world, except in the abodes of the guilty, goes out to the British airmen who, undaunted by odds, unwearied in their constant challenge and mortal danger, are turning the tide of the World War by their prowess and by their devotion. Never in the field of human conflict was so much owed by so many to so few. All hearts go out to the fighter pilots, whose brilliant actions we see with our own eyes day after day; but we must never forget that all the*

time, night after night, month after month, our bomber squadrons travel far into Germany, find their targets in the darkness by the highest navigational skill, aim their attacks, often under the heaviest fire, often with serious loss, with deliberate careful discrimination, and inflict shattering blows upon the whole of the technical and war-making structure of the Nazi power. On no part of the Royal Air Force does the weight of the war fall more heavily than on the daylight bombers, who will play an invaluable part in the case of invasion and whose unflinching zeal it has been necessary in the meanwhile on numerous occasions to restrain.'

Those words may have failed to create an impression in the chamber, in the view of one observer, but there was 'media' reaction the next day. High in its report the *Manchester Guardian* recorded:

'The work of the RAF, both in defence and in offence, has been beyond all expectations and all praise; in a striking sentence he said that "never in the field of human conflict was so much owed by so many to so few". It would not have been Mr Churchill if, while thus encouraging us, he had not insisted on the trials that still await us. The air attack will go on because it must; for the same reason an attempt at invasion must always be expected. Hitler has committed himself deeply to our destruction; let him once show that he is faltering against us, and everyone will know that he and, with him, Mussolini face inevitable defeat. Therefore he will go on attacking so long as his strength lasts.'

Not only did the reference to 'so few' apparently make little impact on many present to hear the speech, but the choice of words and perhaps even of punctuation, has led to debate ever since about the Prime Minister's meaning. So, in drawing attention, to the deeds of a 'few' did Churchill mean aircrew throughout the RAF, fighter pilots only, or fighter pilots and the men of bomber squadrons?

One who had no doubt at the time was Air Chief Marshal Dowding. When he left Fighter Command in November 1940 he wrote to the men he had led:

'My Dear Fighter Boys
'In sending you this, my last message, I wish I could say all that is in my heart. I cannot hope to surpass the simple eloquence of the Prime Minister's

words, "Never before has so much been owed by so many to so few". The debt
remains and will increase.

'In saying good bye to you I want you to know how continually you have
been in my thoughts and that, though our direct connection may be severed, I
may yet be able to help you in your gallant fight.

'Good bye to you and God bless you all.'

Churchill himself had a firm view of the matter, at least in retrospect. In *The*
Second World War, Volume II, Their Finest Hour, he wrote:

'At the summit (of endeavour in the Battle of Britain) the stamina and valour
of our fighter pilots remained unconquerable and supreme. Thus Britain was
saved. Well might I say in the House of Commons, "Never in the field of
human conflict was so much owed by so many to so few".'

The Air Ministry announcement regarding a Battle of Britain Clasp in 1945
confirmed the 'fighter' view of the matter and so 'The Few' has come to be
used generally in the context of the aircrew (not just pilots) of RAF Fighter
Command.

It is perhaps worthy of note that the historic sentence did quickly start to
have some currency.

In his entry for Sunday, 22 September 1940 (precisely a week after 'Battle
of Britain Day') Jock Colville recorded that:

'Sir F. Pile, C-in-C Anti-Aircraft, and General Lock of the War Office, came
to lunch with the Prime Minister at Chequers. Mary Churchill, daughter of
the PM, was also present. During a discussion about the fall of France and
the speed with which Britain had been able to re-orientate itself after this
disaster, Miss Churchill ventured the bon mot, "Never before has so much
been betrayed for so many by so few."'

Colville wrote in a footnote, *'At that time variations on this theme had not become*
as fashionable as they did subsequently.'

Chapter Two

The Route to The Clasp

With the hindsight of seven decades, perhaps three main wartime strands of demand for recognition of the Battle of Britain can be discerned.

There was the view that a list should be made of the Allied airmen who flew in the battle. There was the campaign to gain them an emblem to wear. There was also strongly held opinion that some memorial to 'The Few' should be established. While the proponents of all three ideas held broadly common cause, different people channelled their energies, ideas, resources and contacts towards varied objectives.

Problems of definition arose from the start. Had there been a Battle of Britain? If so, how should it be defined? Churchill had created the legend of The Few, but who were these men? Looking at a squadron roll or a photograph of a group of personnel, how might some of them be defined as members of this new and exclusive club, while others were rejected from the historic honour of being considered participants in the Battle of Britain? Three quarters of a century after the event, all these matters are still hotly debated, even if people tend to accept that the framework is in place. Certainly, in terms of official pronouncement, there is no doubt.

In the years of war that followed the events of 1940 there was a strong feeling in many quarters that the questions needed to be addressed despite the obstacles to doing so in wartime. Yet the difficulty of the circumstances was great. 'Jock' Colville, private secretary to the Prime Minister and an RAF pilot himself (though with no claim to being of The Few), was surely not alone when he wondered in his diary whether there was too much concern about awards before the war had been won.

This was far from being the only issue. Now the fact that the war ended in 1945 is understood. It does not need to be reconsidered in any discussion. At the beginning of that year there was no certainty that hostilities (especially in the Far East) would have ceased by its end. There was even less means of accurate prediction on the subject in earlier years. There could easily have been a need to announce a 1939–1944 Star or a 1939–1946 award, rather than the award that actually came about. Further victories might have led to cases being made on behalf of the participants in those events for recognition by a campaign award.

Moving back as far as 1941 we find two significant documents that started the process of defining the Battle of Britain and those who took part.

In March 1941 appeared the Air Ministry pamphlet *Battle of Britain* which was written anonymously by Hilary St George Saunders. No doubt there was editing of this work 'by committee' but Saunders was very early in the field, after Winston Churchill, in defining the battle.

Saunders, who lived from 1898 to 1951, had worked for the Secretariat of the League of Nations for a year before the war. He served on Lord Mountbatten's staff and held the posts of Assistant Librarian and then Librarian of the House of Commons. He was the anonymous author of a number of the pamphlets which kept the British public informed of the doings of the RAF in the war. He was credited as co-author, with Denis Richards, of the three-volume HMSO publication, *The Royal Air Force 1939–45*, which appeared between 1953 and 1955.

In addition Saunders was a leading candidate for authorship of the official work, which eventually appeared in 1961 in four volumes as *The Strategic Air Offensive Against Germany 1939–45*, from the pens of Noble Frankland and Sir Charles Webster. However Saunders was not appointed to the task, with his poor health at the time and his lack of credentials as an historian being crucial factors. His writing output also included a novel and a biography of Robert Baden-Powell, founder of the scout movement.

In one sense at least the view of the Battle of Britain constructed by this authority lacked permanence. The Air Ministry document divided the battle into four phases, which began on 8 August 1940 and ended on 31 October of that year. The starting date was perfectly tenable. It was the day on which took place what became known to the RAF as The Battle of Convoy Peewit as the convoy (CW9 to the Navy) sailed westwards along the English Channel. The ships were frequently assailed both by the Luftwaffe and by E-boats of the Kriegsmarine. After that Thursday the focus of the fighting gradually moved inland from the Channel, giving people at ground level a much greater view of the struggle which was taking place.

This official account concluded with the words demonstrating how the historic importance of the battle was already recognised, *'Future historians may compare (the Battle of Britain) with Marathon, Trafalgar and the Marne.'*

Five months after the uncredited Saunders had gone into print on the subject, Sir Hugh Dowding completed a traditional task for generals who have fought a battle or a campaign and submitted his despatch on the Battle of Britain.

On the question of the starting date Dowding was of a different opinion. He did write that, *'there are grounds for choosing the date of 8th August, on which was made the first attack in force against laid objectives in this country as the beginning of the Battle.'* However, Dowding pointed out that the German assaults on convoys in July had not merely been intended to sink British shipping, but to draw the RAF up to fight. Therefore, in the view of the former Air Officer Commanding in Chief of Fighter Command, this phase of the fighting had to be taken into account in fixing dates retrospectively.

Dowding went on:

'I have therefore, somewhat arbitrarily, chosen the events of the 10th July as the opening of the Battle. Although many attacks had previously been made on convoys, and even on land objectives such as Portland, the 10th July saw the employment by the Germans of the first really big formation (70 aircraft) intended primarily to bring our Fighter Defence to battle on a large scale.'

Though this was far from the last that would be heard on the issue of dates, the Dowding view was eventually set in stone.

In considering the suitability of 10 July as a starting date for the Battle of Britain it is worth noting that there was some slight sense, on the day itself, that its historic importance should be stated.

Speaking in the House of Commons, Sir Edward Grigg, Joint Parliamentary Under Secretary at the War Office, said:

'This afternoon one of the greatest air battles of the war has been going on. At this moment it may be that bombers are over many of our towns. Tonight thousands of our soldiers will be on the alert waiting for an attack which may come in several places at dawn.'

As we now know, Grigg, a former Governor of Kenya and the future Lord Altrincham, was wrong about the imminence of an invasion attempt, but his words do rather support the Dowding view of the start date. So the existence of a battle had been established. Now a key question to be dealt with was the award, if any, to be given to the men who had taken part in this campaign which had entered everyday vocabulary.

Nevertheless, the idea of 8 August as the starting point of the battle persisted in many minds through the war years and well beyond. As recently as 2004, the *Daily Telegraph* obituary of Group Captain John Peel, who had commanded No 145 Squadron in the battle, attributed to him the firing of the battle's first shots – on 8 August.

So important was the question of who should be given emblems, and for what wartime service, that MPs fretted frequently over the matter as did senior officers in all three services.

The Army had perhaps won a victory in terms of awards, when the Africa Star had been announced in July 1943 despite the war continuing. Many had noted the apparent anomaly that the accompanying Eighth Army Clasp was not awarded for service before 23 October 1942, the start of the second, and more famous, Battle of El Alamein. Men who had died in action under generals who had preceded Montgomery were not to be recipients.

Plans for a 1939 to 1943 Star were announced early in 1944. Broadly, it was intended that it should be worn by officers and other ranks of United Kingdom and Colonial Forces who did not qualify for the Africa Star and who had aggregated six months of service in a number of overseas theatres, including time spent as a prisoner of war. Six months of service in 'dangerous waters' counted. Members of the Women's Auxiliary Territorial Service and the Voluntary Aid Detachment were included. The Africa Star was regarded as the senior award and the intention was that nobody should wear both that and the 1939 to 1943 Star.

On 22 March 1944 preparations for D-Day were well advanced and, in Italy, the Battle of Monte Cassino was inflicting casualties and would do so for some time to come. Despite this it was decided that Parliamentary time should be devoted to awards including that of the 1939–1943 Star and the Africa Star.

In his speech during the 22 March debate Mr Churchill addressed the issue of worthy people who might be excluded from awards. The debate in this area continues now, so many years later. He said:

'The most difficult border line case is, of course, the anti-aircraft battery, and especially the Dover coastal batteries, which are constantly engaged with the enemy's artillery across the Straits. I have been most anxious to include these batteries in the 1939–43 ribbon. Up to the present I have found no way of doing so without opening the door, successively, first to the whole of the Ack-ack Command and, secondly, to the searchlights and predictors of all kinds, without which the guns cannot fire or cannot hit, and whose personnel were and still often are, in equal danger to that of the gunners. In the next place you would immediately come to the National Fire Service, whose casualties have been at a much heavier rate than the ack-ack batteries.

'And, then, what about the Police, who stood around and kept order and rendered every assistance? And what about the ARP and the fire guards so often in danger and discharging their work with so much efficiency as we can see even from our recent minor experiences? If the National Fire Service and others like them were included, how could the whole Regular Army which stood in Great Britain be excluded, or the Dominion Forces which performed here a vital strategic role? If the Regular Army were included, why should not the Home Guards be eligible, who did their work without pay at the end of long days, who wore their uniforms and played an essential part in hurling back the danger of invasion from our shores? There remain a number of other categories such as the training and maintenance personnel of the RAF, the bomb disposal squads, which is, with the ack-ack batteries, one of the balancing cases. In many cases personal decorations have been won on a large scale by that heroic band of men, but, at the same time, I am admitting quite frankly the difficulties which these cases have created—the difficulty of denying and the difficulty of opening the door almost to a very vast extent.'

Later, responding to an intervention from Lady Astor, the Prime Minister drew attention to yet more deserving cases and the difficulty of appropriately recognising them. He commented:

'But if these grants were made so widespread, could you stop at the Services themselves? Indeed, I think the civil population, the railwaymen, who bore with immense composure and unflinching fortitude the full fury of the blitz and went about their ordinary work with faithful diligence and punctuality under the most trying conditions and those who continued in factories at work while the danger signals were going, would certainly have a moral claim to be *considered. If danger is to be made the test, if proper and correct demeanour in the face of danger, and showing indifference to personal injury or life, if that is to be made the test, millions of civilian men and women in their small homes with nothing but the Anderson or Morrison shelters to shield them— not that I deprecate those admirable institutions—who all the time preserved so fine a spirit, they would have a claim as against the men in uniform ...'*

The day's discussion about eligibility rumbled on. Amongst those to contribute to the debate was Sir Lambert Ward Bt, Conservative member for Hull North West who had served in the Honourable Artillery Company and commanded the Howe Battalion of the Royal Naval Division in the First World War. He remarked that:

'it is rather difficult to understand why the ARP services, the National Fire Service, the Home Guard and other services which fought in the blitz in cities like London, Liverpool and Hull should not be qualified to receive these distinctions, when one thinks of the fact that many people, at Cairo for example, are to receive the most coveted decoration of all, the Africa Star, when, in many cases, they have not experienced a single shell, shot or bomb. It is not too much to say that the greatest danger that they have been called upon to face is the danger of an ill-prepared dinner at Shepheards Hotel. When one thinks of the casualties incurred by men in the ARP services in Hull and in the East End of London, it seems unfair that they should not be entitled to receive what people who have passed the whole of the war in Cairo, where they have boasted in letters of the good time they are having, are entitled to receive.'

A large number of other MPs spoke. A contribution of particular note in the history of the commemoration of the Battle of Britain came from Sir Ronald Ross Bt, the member for Londonderry, who declared:

'Notoriously in all Service matters there is nothing more difficult than that of the award of decorations. As many will remember, André Maurois in the last war described how shells and decorations descended alike upon the just and upon the unjust. But there is one thing we must always remember that, as was said in a famous British comic opera: "When everybody's somebody then no one's anybody". If you disperse the decoration too widely, it ceases to have

any great value. In the course of the discussion, to which I have listened with very great interest, there have been various suggestions, but I would only make one comment upon them. Having had some association with the Anti-Aircraft Defence of Great Britain at one time, I think that the allocation of a similar award for the anti-aircraft personnel and for the civil personnel would not be at all satisfactory and there would be very grave difficulties in carrying it out without producing ill-feeling and a sense of hardship amongst various people.

'We have acknowledged that those who won the great victory of North Africa shall have upon the ribbon of their African medal a particular distinction. Now that battle was undoubtedly one of the turning points of the war but, on the other hand, there was another battle which was an even more significant turning point in the war, and the men who were the spearhead which won that battle have never received the slightest recognition in the shape of an award as a separate body. I refer to the fighter pilots of the Battle of Britain. They have had from the Prime Minister the most unexampled tribute that any body of fighting men have ever had, but has that been translated into something which shall be visible to those who meet them in the street? No. In my submission, they should be entitled to wear some emblem upon their 1939–43 Star which would make it plain that they were the fighter pilots of the Battle of Britain. We know what we owe to them.

'It is fitting that I, a member of another Service, should make this suggestion, which I think will have the support of nearly everybody in this House. We are, and I think few of us are exceptions to the rule, somewhat affected by the numbers of people involved, perhaps the numbers of our constituents, perhaps the number of people in the country at large. We have had many suggestions in the course of this Debate which would involve the issue of medals to tens of thousands and, perhaps unwittingly, we have rather multiplied the claim by the number who claim it. Well, the people I am putting forward are unaffected by that. There are very few survivors left of that gallant band.'

Major Sir Jocelyn Lucas (Portsmouth, South): *'About 100.'*
Sir R. Ross:

'I do not suppose there are 100. None of them has approached me and I do not suppose that any one of them has approached any other Member of this House, because that is not the sort of men they are. If we take two standards

as regards the award of a star, which is a peculiar decoration, and if we measure up the special claims of the fighter pilots, I think they have an unexampled priority. Let us first of all think what value their services were to the country. We have the tribute of the right hon. Gentleman the Prime Minister to that, a tribute which has never been questioned by anyone – that never was so much owed by so many to so few. Then let us consider the second standard by which the award of a decoration may be measured, the personal risk, the added peculiar danger. We think of these young men going up, their squadrons scrambling into the air to meet a number of hostile aircraft that would sometimes be described simply as 200 plus, and think of 12 or nine or even six machines unhesitatingly attacking formations, however large and formidable.

'I think that anyone who has been privileged to see the combat film of the early war in the air will never forget it. The gallantry was there, the service was there, and I would urge as strongly as possible that these survivors of the gallant band, which saved the country and won the first signal victory over Germany, should be entitled to one little piece of metal to wear upon the ribbon which would show that there was a man who was a fighter pilot in the Battle of Britain.'

(Sir Jocelyn Lucas, 4th Baronet, whose estimate of the number of survivors of The Few proved to be somewhat wide of the mark, was the Conservative MP for Portsmouth South. He had served in the Royal Warwickshire Regiment and earned the MC. He bred Sealyham Terriers and the Lucas Terrier variant, a cross with a Norfolk Terrier, was named after him.)

Later Commander Peter Agnew, Conservative member for Camborne, Cornwall, commented:

'The suggestion has been made that fighter pilots should have a special rosette to be added to their 1939–43 Ribbons. Surely a way ought to be found, after the Prime Minister has put all our thoughts into words in his classic phrase about the work they did, to record that visibly on their ribbons so that that small band of individuals, as they now are, can be distinguished in that way.'

(Agnew had served in the Royal Navy between the wars, including on the Royal Yacht *Victoria and Albert*. He returned to the service as the Second World War was about to begin, commanding the destroyer HMS *Ramsey*. He became an assistant government whip. His Parliamentary constituency was later abolished but he returned to the House as MP for South Worcestershire, retiring in 1966. He died in 1990.)

Sir Ronald Ross followed up quickly on this debate by writing to Sir Archibald Sinclair, at the Air Ministry, making the case for an award to the Battle of Britain airmen.

The reply from Sinclair, dated 2 April 1944, while reflecting the mood of the parliamentary debate by stressing the need for consideration to be given to other groups, assured Ross that his view was that The Few deserved to receive some recognition.

> '*I need hardly say that I cordially agree with you that the Battle of Britain ought to be especially commemorated by the award of a star or clasp and I have every hope that something of the kind will be done eventually,*' he wrote.

Sinclair took the matter further and the Air Ministry made the case to the Committee on the Grant of Honours, Decorations and Medals.

At this point the considerable discussion on which campaigns should be recognised visibly and the inter-service debate and political argument was intensifying. The job of coming up with recommendations on the who, what, where and when fell to the Committee on the Institution of Honours, Decorations and Medals in Time of War, which, it is clear from the official records, was heavily influenced in its deliberations by the opinions of the Prime Minister.

One of Mr Churchill's oft expressed views could be summed up as the idea that the mass of RAF personnel on the ground incurred no more danger than the civilians who tried to live their lives in blitzed towns. Their contribution to the war effort was to support a relatively small band of heroic pilots. In the Prime Minister's mind there appeared to be a difference between those such as anti-aircraft and coastal artillery gunners who engaged the enemy and those whose role did not involve the discharge of weapons.

The committee, mainly comprised of civil servants, does not seem to have felt itself powerful enough to argue with such a high authority on the question of RAF groundcrew. At the end of the war the situation was that the anti-aircraft and coastal gunners did not get the 1939–1945 Star (which had naturally replaced the 1939 to 1943 award) and neither did the RAF groundcrew.

Nonetheless, few could argue against recognition of The Few. On 24 May 1945 Air Ministry Order, A.532/1945 announced with brevity that there would be a clasp to the 1939–45 Star to be worn by men who had been in the crews of fighter aircraft during the Battle of Britain. Thus, from the outset, it was made clear that the award was limited to aircrew and to those who had served in fighters.

There was at that stage no indication of who precisely, amongst the aircrew of Fighter Command would be entitled to put up the clasp. The confusion which was to become a part of the history of the clasp was given an early boost when the dates for the battle were stated in a command paper as 1 July to 31 October 1940.

Further information came in another Air Ministry Order on 23 July 1945 (AMO A.741/1945) which in part stated that:

'Issues of silver-gilt rose emblems denoting a Clasp to the 1939–45 Star may be made to aircrew personnel who flew in fighter aircraft engaged in the Battle of Britain between 10th July 1940 and 31st October 1940. Issues are to be confined to those who operated with the undermentioned squadrons:

'Nos 1, 17, 19, 23, 25, 29, 32, 41, 43, 46, 53, 54, 56, 59, 64, 65, 66, 72, 73, 74, 79, 85, 87, 92, 111, 141, 145, 151, 152, 213, 219, 222, 229, 234, 235, 236, 238, 242, 249, 253, 257, 264, 266, 302, 303, 310, 312, 401 (No 1 RCAF Squadron), 501, 504, 600, 601, 602, 603, 604, 605, 607, 609, 610, 611, 615 and 616 ...

'COs are not to admit claims for this highly-prized emblem which are open to any possible doubt. The Clasp is not available for personnel who flew in aircraft other than fighters, notwithstanding that they may have been engaged with the enemy in the air during the qualifying period.'

As we will see this did not end the matter as far as qualifying units were concerned, but it did remove in its detail any conceivable doubt about the fact that (rightly or wrongly) only a very select band of fighter aircrew qualified. The wartime discussions in Parliament and elsewhere had raised the hopes of other groups and some of the people involved, who had served under the auspices of Fighter Command and elsewhere, might well have had a justifiable grievance.

Since 1945 the clasp has been worn on occasions, and amongst others, by personnel of Bomber Command, the Women's Auxiliary Air Force and Royal

Navy men engaged in rescue operations. The AMO of July 1945 destroyed any case they might put forward for entitlement. There was no ambiguity.

There appears to have been no need to have mentioned No 401 Squadron. In the Battle of Britain it had been No 1 Squadron, RCAF and renumbering to 401 did not take place until 1 March 1941 at Digby.

Nos 302 and 303 were the two Polish squadrons to have flown in the Battle and Nos 310 and 312, the two Czechoslovak squadrons. A number of squadrons normally part of Coastal Command featured on this list, all having been under the control of Fighter Command at some point in 1940.

Further grounds for confusion lay in the fact the Royal Navy personnel had served in the Battle of Britain and the Royal Navy, as is often the case, wished to deal with things in its own way. In 1945 two Admiralty Fleet Orders (2686 and 3115) detailed the award of the clasp to those wearing dark blue.

There was an interval of less than a year from the July 1945 AMO before further change to the definition of who qualified for the clasp was promulgated in another AMO, this one being A.544/1946 issued on 24 June that year.

As a result of this AMO aircrew who had flown operationally with No 248 Squadron (another of those whose home was Coastal Command), as well as with the Fighter Interception Unit became recipients. However, the new AMO deleted Nos 53 and 59 Squadrons from the list, apparently partly on the grounds that these squadrons flew Blenheim IV bombers, whereas the Blenheim squadrons that remained on the accredited list had operated fighter variants. In addition, it appears that both squadrons had ceased to be under Fighter Command control in early July before the official date for the start of the battle.

The Fighter Interception Unit had been established in April 1940, with the purpose of developing new technology, including early airborne intercept radar. Equipped with Blenheims, Beaufighters and Hurricanes, the FIU did indeed see action in the battle.

So, having been told that they were entitled to the clasp, former aircrew of Nos 53 and 59 Squadrons now found that they were not entitled. Or did they? Many years later some people affected by this ruling claimed that it was only in 1960 that they were told of their change of status.

It is worth noting that a painting currently held by the RAF Museum, Hendon illustrates the point. The striking portrait produced in 1945 by Alfred Egerton Cooper (1883–1974) shows Group Captain Clair Grece who had served with No 59 Squadron at the time of the Battle of Britain. His 1939–1945 Star has the rosette indicating clasp entitlement.

In addition, at least one of the men concerned was able to quote a letter from RAF personnel confirming his entitlement, although there have been plenty of instances over the years of letters from service personnel departments not sticking to the laid down definition when pronouncing on eligibility for the clasp.

Presumably a considerable proportion of those affected had left the service in 1945 and 1946 and it must be considered doubtful that the trouble was taken to send them copies of the June 1946 AMO.

Officially the matter rested at the point of the 1946 ruling until the twentieth anniversary of the battle in 1960 was approaching. The AMOs issued a decade and a half earlier had had the effect of leaving the Westminster Abbey Roll of Honour and memorial window out on a limb (see Chapter 4). The divergence of definitions used had been noticed and there was correspondence addressed to the Abbey and the Ministry of Defence relating to aircrew who had not been included on the Abbey roll, which, in any case, also featured the names of men who had not qualified for the clasp under the Air Ministry rulings.

A minute was circulated by Air Member for Personnel on 29 August 1960 drawing attention to the difficulty and proposing modifications.

At the heart of this minute was written:

'I have had a thorough investigation carried out into the omission of certain squadrons and units which took part in the Battle of Britain from the AMO issued in 1946 and the Memorial Window in Westminster Abbey.

'I am now satisfied that:

'Nos 3, 232, 245, 247 and 263 Squadrons included in the Abbey window but omitted from the AMO;

'Nos 235, 236 and 248 and the Fighter Interception Unit included in the AMO but omitted from the Abbey window, and

'Nos 421 and 422 Flights omitted from both the window and the AMO all took part in the Battle of Britain.'

This document resulted in a new AMO (N.850/1960), dated 9 November which put into effect the changes listed in the 29 August minute. A major contributor to the research from which this minute was drafted was Group Captain Tom Gleave of the Battle of Britain Fighter Association. During 1959 and 1960 Gleave, working at the Cabinet Office at the time, had delved into, amongst others, operations record books, Cabinet documents, Lord

Dowding's despatch, the AMO of 1946 and the Westminster Abbey Roll of Honour.

Even with the 1960 AMO, the tinkering was not finished. The number of squadrons and other units designated as 'Battle of Britain' was now sixty-nine. In 1961 the figure familiar today of seventy-one was reached with the addition to the official list of Nos 804 and 808 Naval Air Squadrons. So men who had flown within the Fleet Air Arm were now entitled to receive the clasp, as some of their FAA comrades, who had flown on attachment with Fighter Command squadrons, had been since the start.

Neither 804 or 808 had been anywhere near the thick of the action during the battle but they had nevertheless been attached to Fighter Command at a relevant time. This then was the point at which the definition of the battle and its Allied participants was arrived at that remained in force in 2014.

Probably all similar military definitions are as arbitrary as this one and therefore as potentially controversial. It is possible to make a case for extending the dates or contracting them. There are a number of units on the list of seventy-one which, as things turned out, saw no action or very little action in No 13 Group between 10 July and 31 October, while different squadrons were heavily engaged and suffering high casualty rates flying from such airfields as Kenley, Biggin Hill, Gravesend, Tangmere and Hornchurch.

There were men who joined those squadrons in October 1940 and took part in very little fighting compared with their new comrades who had become veterans in August and September.

An example of the difficulties is provided by No 263 Squadron which had been re-established at Drem, near North Berwick, on 10 June 1940 after suffering disastrously in the Norwegian campaign, including through the sinking of the aircraft carrier HMS *Glorious*. During the Battle of Britain the squadron operated from Drem and Grangemouth with detachments to other Scottish airfields. Hurricanes replaced the Gladiators it had lost as a result of its Norwegian involvement and it was also given the task of evaluating the first operational Westland Whirlwind.

The late Wing Commander John Young, as archivist of the BBFA, corresponded with an officer who had served with 263 Squadron at the time. John Young pointed out to him that he was entitled to apply for the clasp and membership of the BBFA. The officer concerned declined on the grounds that whereas he was technically so qualified, he could not bring himself to wear the clasp or join the BBFA and stand alongside men who had been involved in the heavy fighting in the south of England, while he had been in Scotland in relative safety.

At least one other 263 Squadron pilot took the same line and the same view was expressed in recent years by a former naval officer whose posting at the time of the battle to Castletown in the north of Scotland, with an FAA squadron, made him entitled to the award.

That naval pilot went on to earn a DSO flying from HMS *Ark Royal* in the Mediterranean, so he saw intense action in the Second World War, but he was not in the presence of the enemy during the Battle of Britain.

A further issue that has caused controversy over the years is the matter of whether operational sorties were 'authorised'. The word is not generally used in the AMOs, but it is implicit in those orders. Clearly if a sortie was not properly authorised and recorded, certainly in the person's logbook, or his pilot's and preferably in the squadron's operations record book, it would be very difficult to verify it.

There has always been a feeling of some unfairness about the fact that some qualified for the clasp who had not been in action in the battle and others who did see action did not receive the clasp. At one end of the debate, as already indicated, are those who flew, perhaps on a patrol, with one of the designated units and at the correct time, did not see the enemy and, despite that, are entitled to the clasp.

At the other end of this discussion are a small number of men who did fly into action, or at least operationally, in fighters in the battle, but were not entitled to wear the clasp or join the BBFA. The problem here is that, at the time, they were not with one of the seventy-one accredited units. In most cases they were instructors with operational training units who used available Hurricanes or Spitfires to search for the enemy and perhaps locate and even shoot down that enemy. They had generally flown at the request of and under the instructions of a Fighter Command controller, who may well have vectored them towards the enemy.

Be that as it may, they are not officially Battle of Britain airmen. The split hair here rankles to this day with some of the airmen involved and with some families.

The son of one of these former instructors approached the Battle of Britain Memorial Trust in 2011 about the possibility of adding his father's name to the Christopher Foxley-Norris Memorial Wall at Capel-le-Ferne. Though the matter was considered by the trustees, there was perhaps little doubt about the outcome.

The subsequent reply sent by Group Captain Patrick Tootal in his capacity as Secretary of the Trust said:

'1) Your father clearly had a very gallant war record including playing a part in the defence of Britain in 1940.

'2) The policy of the Memorial Trust – and of the Battle of Britain Fighter Association and the Air Historical Branch – has always been to keep to the definition of the Battle promulgated in AMOs …

'3) The Trust and the Clasp holders themselves have always recognised that many men and women in all three services, as well as civilians, contributed to the ending of the Nazi invasion threat.

'4) There were various groups of people who might have qualified for the Clasp had a slightly different definition been established. Indeed members of Nos 53 and 59 Squadrons and those in the 71 units who flew operationally only between July 1 and July 9 1940 would for a time have been under the impression that they were to receive the Clasp.

'After careful consideration the Trustees concluded that the present situation must be maintained, with the names on the Christopher Foxley-Norris Memorial Wall being strictly those who qualified for the Battle of Britain Clasp.

'I appreciate that this was not the response that you were hoping for, but I trust that you can accept that the issue is complex and that changing the definition for inclusion on the Wall now, particularly unilaterally, would create many problems.'

So there have been a variety of issues relating to people who might feel morally entitled to the clasp, might have been told in the early days that they were entitled to it or perhaps have erroneously worn it through misunderstanding.

In an entirely different league are the men who have claimed to have qualified for the clasp where there is no basis in fact whatsoever.

The problem began early on. In 1949, for instance, a book called *Engines over London* was published in London by Carroll & Nicholson. The author, Lewis Whitnell, gave an account of his wartime experiences in the RAF, including flying Hurricanes with No 85 Squadron in the Battle of Britain.

Marshal of the Royal Air Force Lord Douglas of Kirtleside contributed an introduction.

The book raised eyebrows. What is true in Whitnell's story and what is not is difficult to work out. He seems to have been on No 85 Squadron for a spell during the Battle of Britain, and then on No 249 Squadron, before returning to No 85. However, there is no evidence of an operational flight with either squadron and consequently no evidence that Lewis Whitnell qualified for the clasp.

Action was swift when doubts were raised. The initial print run of *Engines Over London* was withdrawn. A new version appeared without the introduction by Lord Douglas, with reference to it on the jacket removed and a disclaimer inside in red which ran:

> '*The publishers wish to state that since publication it has become clear that the author of this book did not take part in a number of the incidents in which he claims to have participated, although he gives a vivid and realistic description of the Battle of Britain. The manuscript was accepted by the publishers in good faith; and in view of the fact that it is considered to contain some of the most thrilling accounts of aerial combat ever written, they have decided to continue with the publication of this book. They nevertheless felt it right to issue this disclaimer as they cannot in the light of their discovery guarantee the authenticity of all the facts. With this proviso, the book can be recommended to give the 'feel' of those splendid days of 1940 from the point of view of the pilots who risked or gave their lives.*
>
> '*In the book as originally issued, Lord Douglas of Kirtleside had contributed an introduction. As soon as the information previously referred to became known, at Lord Douglas's request, his introduction was withdrawn from the book.*'

The book is indeed a thumping good read, but it cannot be relied on as a statement of historical fact and the name of Lewis Whitnell will not be found on any official modern list of Battle of Britain airmen.

Many years after the publication of *Engines Over Britain*, the problem of false claims to entitlement remains.

One of the sadder stories is the man who was in the habit of appearing at the war memorial in Gravesend, Kent for the Remembrance service in November. On these occasions he wore the clasp. When questioned as to his qualification his story was superficially credible, yet, on the least examination, clearly untrue.

Equally disconcerting in its way was the case of the family of a man who had maintained to them until his death that he had served with a Spitfire squadron in the battle and had flown into action. Apparently he had given them vivid accounts of aerial combat. The family expressed indignation that his name did not appear on the Christopher Foxley-Norris Memorial Wall at Capel-le-Ferne, the London Monument and so on.

Part of the story was true. Investigation showed that the man had served on the squadron in the battle, but in a ground trade. He had played an important part in winning the Battle of Britain, but he had not qualified for the clasp, despite what he had told his family. Inevitably this was a name that was not added to memorial wall or monument.

Nor was the name added of the RAF pilot whose funeral in Yorkshire some years ago was conducted on the basis that he had flown in the Battle of Britain, though he had not. Gullible regional journalists printed the stories of combat in 1940 with which he had entertained his family. National media did some checking and discovered the truth.

Another with no claim to the clasp recorded his memories of the battle, including being shot down in a Hurricane, for the East Midlands Oral History Archive.

In the end the only likely route now to being recognised as one of The Few for an airman is for his name to appear in a unit's Operations Record Book (forms 540 and 541). An alternative might be an entry in an individual's logbook signed at the bottom of the page by the CO or Flight Commander. Wartime conditions meant that ORBs were not always kept with assiduity and some were destroyed. If properly kept, Form 541 should record the names of aircrew, with initials and rank (though this often proves to be expecting too much), and the operational and non-operational sorties that they flew. Postings in and out are amongst the information to be found in form 540.

Regular traps that have led to mistakes in compiling lists of battle participants are Form 541 entries where a common surname appears with no initials as well as the misspelling of unusual or foreign names. Bad handwriting plays its part in frustrating the compilation of a complete list of The Few.

The case of Sergeant William Gerald Silver of No 152 Squadron is a pointer to the difficulties. In the 1970s the BBFA took the view for a time that his name should be removed from the list of battle participants because reference to him had not been found in the squadron's ORB. This decision was quickly rescinded and rightly so. Not only did Bill Silver fly operationally in the battle, he was shot down and killed over Portsmouth on 25 September 1940.

Silver's death in action was seen by his comrade Pilot Officer 'Boy' Marrs who, in a letter to his father, later published in *The Aeroplane* (21 September 1945), declared that Silver's Spitfire, 'dived vertically into the sea', having been jumped by a Messerschmitt Bf 109. Marrs reflected that, *'It shows how careful one must be to watch one's tail.'*

However, the University of London academic, Dr Tony Mansell, was right to point out that:

> *'The important thing to realise about Forms 540 and 541, and especially the latter, is that they were being compiled on airfields which could be in the thick of the fighting, including being bombed, and their compilers had other things on their minds than the convenience of future historians.'*

Partly for the same reason logbooks cannot be entirely relied on either. The leader of The Dam Busters, Wing Commander Guy Gibson, (who missed qualifying for the clasp by about three weeks with No 29 Squadron) was a classic example of an RAF pilot whose logbook does not tell the entire story of his RAF career. He felt he had more important things to do than compile a punctilious record of every flight.

Increasingly, the development of knowledge of who was entitled to the clasp came from sources outside the official channels. The arrival on the scene of another important figure in the story was described by Dr Jeremy Crang in his article in *War & Society* in 2005.

Crang wrote:

> *'Although there was now an official list of the names of the 'few' who had died during the battle, there was still no complete record of the names of all those who had taken part. This was to be provided by Flight Lieutenant John Holloway. In 1940 Holloway had been a sergeant wireless fitter with 615 Squadron and had come greatly to admire the spirit and courage of the pilots who fought in the battle. In 1955 he was stationed at RAF Kenley when the film* Reach for the Sky [the life story of Group Captain Douglas Bader, who had commanded No 242 Squadron in the battle, based on a book by

Paul Brickhill] *was being filmed there and he took the opportunity to collect some of the autographs of the 'few'. Over the following months this became an obsession and Holloway had soon collected over a hundred signatures. A senior officer at Kenley then suggested to him that a collection of all the signatures of the celebrated group would become a most valuable museum piece. Holloway decided to take up the challenge.'*

John Holloway showed remarkable tenacity in his self appointed task. He realised the difficulty of dealing with a group of people of whom no adequate list existed. He quickly contacted Group Captain Tom Gleave, based at the Cabinet Office and through him came to know J.C. Nerney, head of the RAF's Air Historical Branch from its re-establishment in 1941 to 1958.

There was scepticism from the AHB over the likelihood that a comprehensive list could be drawn up, a doubt that the events of the years since have more than justified, but assistance was readily given. John Holloway spent four years scouring the records for qualifying names. Help with incomplete names was given by the RAF records organization.

In 1961 the task that Holloway had imposed on himself was complete to his satisfaction. His list appeared that year as an appendix in the book *The Narrow Margin*, an outstanding account of the Battle of Britain by Derek Wood and Derek Dempster, which has been much republished and reprinted since.

With the benefit of over fifty more years of research by many people, we now know that, inevitably, there were plenty of flaws in the Holloway list. However, his defining of The Few was a remarkable achievement and has provided the basis for serious research ever since.

At this point, John Holloway had already been acknowledged for some time as the expert on the subject and was being frequently consulted by the BBFA on the eligibility of applicants for membership.

An example is the letter dated 6 August 1959 from Wing Commander Bobby Oxspring on behalf of the Association to Holloway. Amongst a number of queries about eligibility Oxspring wrote: '*Gieves* [the tailor] *has issued a tie to Squadron Leader R. Carnall, who says he was a Sergeant Pilot in 111 Squadron from February 1937 to August 1940. Is he OK?*' Holloway was able to confirm that Ralph Carnall indeed qualified as one of The Few.

A less straightforward case in the BBFA files relates to a pilot who had served with one of the qualifying Blenheim squadrons in the battle.

The correspondence is not all available but it appears that this former officer had been encouraged to apply for membership of the association and to attend a reunion, but his qualification was then queried and Holloway was asked to adjudicate.

What Holloway seems to have discovered is that the pilot had flown operationally before the battle, but had been injured in a landing accident and declared temporarily unfit for flying duties. Nonetheless he had twice unofficially flown during the battle as an observer, with two different pilots.

Holloway ruled against allowing the man into association membership. His reasoning appears to have been that as this keenness was kept from the CO and did not feature in the squadron records, the two flights in the battle failed the test because they were unauthorised.

The would-be association member received this verdict with good grace. He had, after all, not realised that he might be entitled to join until he was pushed to apply.

Crang in his article pointed out how Holloway's fascination with the subject went on. He wrote:

'Holloway continued with his autograph collecting. He believed [in 1961] *that approximately 1600 of the "few" were still living and he wrote to all those he could trace to obtain their signatures. He also attended Battle of Britain reunions and made many personal visits to aircrew. On one occasion he travelled to Uxbridge to request the signature of a pilot who lay on his death-bed in a RAF hospital. On another he arrived in Preston to find his pilot breaking the sound barrier in a prototype fighter. Volunteers were recruited in Canada, Australia, New Zealand and the United States to assist him in collecting the signatures of those living abroad.*

'Holloway believed that his task would not be complete without some attempt to obtain the autographs of those who had died. He thus wrote to next of kin inviting them to send a signature of their loved ones. In response he received many additions to his collection, poignantly harvested from private letters, school books, driving licences, passports, blood donors' certificates, prayer books, and even a menu from a German prisoner-of-war camp. This inevitably opened up old wounds. One mother whose boy had been killed in the battle aged 20, included a grief-stricken tribute to her son: "He was the loveliest and most precious gift that God could bestow on any mortal here on earth and I, his mother, shall mourn him, all the rest of my days." Despite

the heartache most relatives were proud that their sons and husbands had not been forgotten and that their names would appear alongside the living.'

The Holloway collection did not stop at The Few themselves. Sir Winston Churchill was there, as well as R.J. Mitchell, designer of the Spitfire and Sir Sidney Camm, whose many designs for Hawker included the Hurricane.

Eventually John Holloway decided that a suitable tribute to The Few would be to hand his collection of signatures to the Imperial War Museum for safekeeping. The signatures were placed in a leather-bound case with gold engraving, with a BBFA tie secured into the binding. On 21 October 1969 Dr Noble Frankland, Director of IWM, received the treasure from John Holloway.

The BBFA arranged a ceremony in which Holloway was presented by Lord Dowding with a silver Spitfire on an ebony stand, a mark of the exceptional contribution Holloway had made both to recording the history of The Few and to the development of the BBFA.

From 1969 to the present the quest so ably pioneered by John Holloway has been continued.

The work of Kenneth G. Wynn, aided by researchers including Bruce Burton, has led to three editions and a supplementary volume of the book, *Men of the Battle of Britain*, starting in 1989.

When the Battle of Britain Monument in London, unveiled in 2005, was being planned a team came together to decide on the names to be included. Their list, with slight modification, was also used on the Christopher Foxley-Norris Memorial Wall at Capel-le-Ferne.

More details of Ken Wynn's work, the London Monument and the National Memorial at Capel-le-Ferne are given in Chapter 5.

There have been many individual researchers and family members of Battle of Britain airmen who have made their own contributions.

In this century it has been possible, for example, to add the name of Pilot Officer (later Squadron Leader) Charles Alexander 'Alastair' Ogilvy to the lists of Battle of Britain participants, including the Monument and the Foxley-Norris Wall. He died in 1995 and the chain of events began when, after the death of his widow, their daughter Susan examined her father's medals, which proved to include the 1939–1945 Star with Battle of Britain Clasp.

Ogilvy had served with No 610 Squadron in 1940 and had been awarded the clasp, yet his name did not appear during the battle in the poorly kept squadron operations record book. However, his logbook showed that, on 25

October 1940, as the battle was about to reach its official conclusion, Pilot Officer Ogilvy had carried out orders to investigate two 'X-raids' – the term for unidentified aircraft reported by RDF or the Observer Corps.

Olgilvy may not have seen enemy aircraft during those sorties, but he nonetheless qualified to receive the clasp, though he does not appear to have regarded himself as one of The Few.

He went on to fly as a Lancaster pilot with No 622 Squadron in Bomber Command and took part in seventeen operations against the enemy, as well as flying in Operation Manna, dropping supplies to Dutch civilians at the end of the war in Europe and Operation Exodus, when he brought Allied PoWs home from Italy.

An even more recent case of intervention by a relative is that of Sergeant Malcolm Finney Edwards. It was recorded that a Sergeant Edwards had made at least one qualifying flight with No 247 Squadron and 'Sergeant Edwards' appeared on lists of Allied airmen from the battle, but with no initials.

An account of how this situation was changed appeared in the 2013 edition of *1940* magazine, published by the Battle of Britain Memorial Trust.

'A mystery on the Memorial Wall at Capel-le-Ferne and other Battle of Britain lists has been solved. Thanks to James Atkinson approaching Edward McManus who runs the website for the Battle of Britain Monument in London, we now know that the 'Edwards' without initials on the Wall was Sergeant Malcolm Finney Edwards.

'It had been known that 'Edwards' served with No 247 Squadron in the Battle ... following the research carried out by James on his grandfather, including studying his logbook, the initials 'M F' can be added to the Wall.

'Malcolm Edwards, 'Eddie' to his comrades, joined the RAFVR on April 8, 1939 and was allocated the number 745861. After completing his training, he served briefly with No 609 Squadron before being posted, on September 1, 1940, to No 247 Squadron at RNAS Roborough, north of Plymouth. The squadron was the only one, designated as having taken part in the Battle of Britain, which was equipped with Gloster Gladiators, although No 804 Naval Air Squadron, operated the Sea Gladiator variant.

'The Gladiator was, in 1937, the last biplane fighter to be introduced to RAF service. Already obsolete at that point, it nonetheless went on to see considerable service in the Second World War, including in the Norwegian campaign and the defence of Malta.

'*Eddie Edwards had two spells later in the war with No 3 Squadron. On December 29, 1944 he was flying one of four Hawker Tempests on reconnaissance, north of Rheine, Germany. During an attack by German fighters Flight Lieutenant Edwards was shot down and killed, his aircraft crashing outside the town of Spelle. He was buried in the local Catholic cemetery, but now rests in the Reichswald Forest War Cemetery.*'

In 2013 Flight Lieutenant Edwards's medals, including 1939–1945 Star with Battle of Britain Clasp, were received by the family.

An example of the establishment of a clear identity of a Battle of Britain airman comes in the notes compiled by one of the most assiduous seekers after The Few, the late Bruce Burton. He pointed out that David Cooper Mitchell had apparently been confused with Peter Mitchell and wrote:

'*The Commonwealth War Graves Commission confirms that Peter Mitchell's service number was 932483, which shows that he enlisted in the war-time RAFVR in June 1940. The CWGC also records that Mitchell was 20 years old when he died in July 1942, which means that he was only 18 when he enlisted in June 1940. The Gazettes show that he had not previously held a commission, and since he would only have been 17 in July 1939, he would have been too young to have previously enlisted in either Class F of the RAFR or the pre-war RAFVR. Having enlisted in June 1940, he apparently joined 5 OTU at the beginning of August, and joined 65 Squadron on 19 August. These details alone make it clear that Peter Mitchell was not the Sergeant Mitchell who operated with 65 Squadron in 1940.*

'*The first edition of* The Narrow Margin, *using J.H. Holloway's original research, merely records: "Mitchell, Sgt, British, 65 Sqdn". He is first identified as "Sgt P. Mitchell" in the 1969 edition of Frank Mason's* Battle Over Britain, *and in 1989* Men of the Battle of Britain *by Kenneth G. Wynn records him as "Peter Mitchell". The 1990 edition of* The Narrow Margin *then records him as "Sgt P. M. Mitchell".*

'*However, 65 Squadron's ORB merely records that "Sgt Mitchell" joined the squadron from 5 OTU on 19 August, without providing any initials or service number. Form 541 of the ORB shows that Sgt Mitchell flew (continually) with 65 Squadron through to the end of 1940 and into 1941, and on June 30 1941 he damaged a Bf 109. Then the ORB records that Sgt D.C. Mitchell had been commissioned with effect from 26 June 1941. On 21 October 1941*

he destroyed an Me 109, but was himself shot down into the English Channel,
but was rescued some two hours later. The final mention of Mitchell was on
February 6, 1942, when he was posted from 65 Squadron to RAF Debden,
pending a posting overseas. (Unfortunately, Debden's ORB does not record the
location of the unit to which Mitchell was eventually posted.)

The London Gazette records that 748420 Sgt David Cooper Mitchell
was commissioned as 69439 Pilot Officer on June 26 1941. His Airman
service number shows that he enlisted in the RAFVR in May 1939. This is
clearly the 'Sgt Mitchell' who flew with 65 Squadron in 1940, and Peter
Mitchell should be replaced by David Cooper Mitchell.

'Although his whereabouts after February 1942 are not yet known, D.C.
Mitchell had returned to the UK by 1944. The Commonwealth War Graves
Commission records that 69439 F/Lt David Cooper Mitchell, RAFVR,
died on 19 June 1944 at the age of 29 and is buried in Glasgow (Eastwood)
Cemetery. The unit with which he was serving at the time is not recorded.'

David Cooper Mitchell was in fact killed on 19 June 1944 whilst flying in
Spitfire I R 7065 of No 57 OTU which collided with Beaufort W 6540 over
Rayburn Lake, Wingates Moor, Northumberland. The Beaufort landed safely.
He is recorded correctly on the Christopher Foxley-Norris Wall at Capel-le-
Ferne, on the Battle of Britain Monument in London and in the third edition
of *Men of the Battle of Britain*.

For many years the Battle of Britain Clasp was the only clasp that could be worn
with the 1939–45 Star. A very late twist in the story occurred on 26 February 2013
when the Government announced the award of a clasp to be worn with the star by
some aircrew who had flown operationally in Bomber Command.

Eligibility was described in the following terms:

'A Clasp to the 1939–45 Star is granted to the aircrew of Bomber Command
who served for at least sixty days, or completed a tour of operations, on a
Bomber Command operational unit and flew at least one operational sortie
on a Bomber Command operational unit from 3 September 1939 to 8 May
1945, inclusive. The award of the Clasp is to be denoted by a silver rose
Emblem when the ribbon alone is worn.

'Eligibility is extended to those members of Bomber Command aircrew
who did not meet the qualifying criteria due to service being brought to an
end by death, wounds or other disability due to service, service marked by a
gallantry award or taken as a prisoner of war.

> *'Foreign nationals commissioned or enlisted into British or, the then,*
> *Dominion Air Forces (eg Royal Canadian Air Force or Royal Australian*
> *Air Force) are eligible provided the individuals did not receive a similar*
> *award from their own Government.*
>
> *'Eligibility to the Bomber Command Clasp has no effect upon eligibility*
> *for World War Two recognition previously awarded and does not suggest*
> *automatic eligibility for any further awards.'*

There had been much disquiet following the Second World War that various groups had not received a specifically designated campaign award. Bomber Command was often argued to be one of the most significant omissions, though many of the 'Bomber Boys' did receive either the Air Crew Europe award or the France and Germany Star.

Air Chief Marshal Sir Arthur Harris who was Air Officer Commanding in Chief, Bomber Command from 1942 to 1945, argued in particular, that groundcrew should have been recognised. A parallel argument from other quarters was that there should have been an award for Fighter Command groundcrew for service in the Battle of Britain.

The campaign for an award for Bomber Command veterans gained fresh momentum in the run-up to the unveiling in 2012 in Green Park, London, of a memorial to more than 55,000 personnel of the Command who had died as a result of aircrew duties during the Second World War.

At the same time as the Bomber Command Clasp was promulgated an Arctic Star was announced for those in the armed forces and the Merchant Navy who had served above the Arctic Circle during the Second World War. Although this award was intended, in particular, to recognize Royal Navy and Merchant Navy personnel who served on Arctic convoys, some RAF air and ground crew were also eligible.

In terms of the Battle of Britain Clasp the story remained incomplete in 2014 in the sense that, with research continuing, there could still be no definitive list of the Allied airmen who took part and so no firm view of their number. The preparation of the third edition of Ken Wynn's *Men of the Battle of Britain* threw up a surname that needed to be changed, as well as inaccurately recorded given names. There was one man who, the evidence suggested, should be removed from the lists and others for whom a case could be made for inclusion. The research was continuing and it would be reasonable to predict further changes in the years ahead.

Chapter Three

The Battle of Britain Fighter Association

The origins of the Battle of Britain Fighter Association were informal and not always well recorded. A desire to maintain wartime comradeship was a factor and so was the concern that through accident or design there were people wearing the Battle of Britain Clasp who were not entitled to it. A proper organization might be able to do something about that.

Veterans of the battle came together at events such as the inauguration of the chapel in Westminster Abbey and the unveiling of the Rolls-Royce memorial window in Derby. They met without ceremony on other occasions. Many also found themselves in contact because they were still serving in the RAF. Some of those who remained officers in the service took to holding a reunion on 15 September each year.

Little detail of these events appears to have survived, though an account of one held in 1946, and said to be the first, exists in a letter written in 1990 by Flight Lieutenant Derek Smythe, who had been an air gunner on Defiants with No 264 Squadron in 1940. Smythe recorded that the meeting took place at the 'Belfry', West Halkin Street, Belgravia, London with Lord Dowding as the guest of honour. The former AOC gave a brief address. Smythe wrote that he had spoken to Wing Commander Pat Hancock – in 1990 Secretary of the BBFA – to confirm the details, including the year, before writing his letter. There remains an establishment known as The Belfry, and also as Mosimann's Club, at 11b West Halkin Street.

Wing Commander John Young, as BBFA archivist, was clear that such a get-together also occurred in 1947 in London and there was a photograph to prove it. It also appears that not only Lord Dowding, but Sir Keith Park was present on at least some occasions.

There was a London meeting held in 1948 at Shepherd's Hotel with the main intention of establishing some order to the wearing of the clasp, but no formally constituted organization developed as a direct result of these occasions.

From the early 1950s, the regular venue for dinners became Bentley Priory, still then the headquarters of Fighter Command as it had been in 1940. This was the period when Air Marshal Sir Basil Embry was Air Officer Commanding in Chief. Embry will come into this story again later. He seems to have been delighted to welcome The Few back to their spiritual home.

Veterans of the battle who had retired from the service were gradually added to the invitation list. Reference was made to the 'Battle of Britain Pilots Reunion' as an organization and, although the Battle of Britain Fighter Association was still not in existence, it was clearly on the horizon. In 1954, for example, Gieves the tailor (Gieves & Hawkes from 1971) was commissioned to produce a tie for Battle of Britain veterans. Sixty years later the firm continues to provide this service.

When Basil Embry retired from the RAF the annual dinner at Bentley Priory became, for a few years, a cocktail party at Biggin Hill. Then annual events took place at the RAF Club at No 128 Piccadilly in London.

Progress toward the formation of an Association was made during 1957. On August 15 that year a circular was distributed in the name of Air Commodore S.C. (Charles) Widdows, which set out possible objects for such an Association. These objectives were agreed (though not for long) at the coming together on 15 September that year.

In the early discussions the question of the name of the new body figured prominently. Even with a gap of more than half a century it is possible to envisage the problems generated by the need to find a designation that was all encompassing of those entitled to the clasp, excluded those not so entitled, gave sufficient prestige in dealings with the Air Ministry and other official bodies, yet also rolled off the tongue.

Recruitment of members began, though from surviving documents, the idea seems to have been initially that this would be, in the main, a means of formalizing the arrangements for the annual September reunion. A committee came together with Widdows as chairman. He was still in the RAF at that point and serving at the Air Ministry. His appointment reflected not only his standing as a holder of the Battle of Britain Clasp and a squadron commander (No 29 Squadron) during the battle, but the fact that he was currently installed at the heart of RAF affairs, with access to secretarial and other assistance.

On 27 March 1958 Widdows despatched to interested parties 'News Letter No 1' of the Battle of Britain Fighter Association from his Air Ministry address in Whitehall Gardens, London SW1.

Not surprisingly, this document set the tone for the early years of the BBFA and it is appropriate to quote from it at some length. Indeed, from its wording, it is possible to argue that this is as good a date as any to be regarded as the moment when the BBFA formally came into existence.

'Dear Member

'This is the first of what I hope will be a series of news letters. These, I anticipate, will not necessarily be issued at regular intervals but will be sent out from time to time when there is something interesting to say to keep you in touch with what is going on during the period between our annual general meetings.

'A list of those entitled to wear the Battle of Britain Clasp will be forwarded as soon as possible. It will be as complete as can be from the information at present available. In this connection I would like to place on record my grateful thanks and deep appreciation for the excellent work of Flight Lieutenant Holloway who is devoting many hours of study and research on this problem and spending a great deal of his own money in the process. However, I shall be grateful if you yourself would let me know of any errors or omissions which occur to you so that amendment lists can be issued as the need arises.

'Since our last general meeting in September your committee has been giving thought to your agreed proposal to set up a permanent association. You will recall that there was some discussion at the time about its proposed name. Your committee has very carefully considered all aspects of this somewhat complicated point and has finally decided that it shall be known as "The Battle of Britain Fighter Association". This was the last obstacle to be overcome before formally setting ourselves up and it can now be taken that the association is in being.

'You will recall that the objects of the Association tentatively included in my circular of 15th August 1957, were agreed at the meeting held on 15th September following. Your Committee has since revised the order and some of the wording of these objects, but not the substance, and it is hoped you will agree that they are now in their correct order of importance and more specific in their meaning. They are as follows:

- *to look after the welfare of members of the Association and their dependents, in co-operation with the Royal Air Force Benevolent Fund and other charitable and advisory institutions, according to their needs.*
- *to preserve the memory of fighter aircrew who died in the Battle of Britain.*

- *to foster good fellowship amongst members of the Association in perpetuation of the comradeship which existed during the Battle of Britain.*
- *to perform the functions and ceremonies in furtherance of the objects of the Association, and to arrange representation at other appropriate functions and ceremonies to which the Association might be invited.*

'*We are now in the process of an official approach to the Air Council for a grant from the Prize Fund to start us on our way. There is no doubt that this grant will only be made if we can show that we intend to cover our running costs by means of an annual subscription. You will also recall that the proposal for an annual subscription was agreed in principle at the last general meeting and the committee are proceeding to plan on this basis.*

However, the main news which I wish to convey in this letter is that we have been in close touch with the committee of the Reserves Club who have invited us to become non-voting members of their club on a block membership basis for 10.6d. per head of those wanting to join.

This arrangement would give to those of us who subscribe full membership, other than voting rights, and would have three main advantages for the Association as a whole:

It would give us a home which would act as a focal centre for our activities, for meeting each other on a rank-free basis and for making contact generally.

It would give us a firm base administratively as all secretarial and other work would be undertaken by the staff of the Reserves Club. The Secretary, Mr Room, has offered to do the work entailed in his own spare time if he finds this necessary.

It would give us an admirable centre for our actual reunions. It would also be a centre where we can accumulate mementos and other items of historic and sentimental interest.

[The newsletter goes on to detail the location of the Reserves Club off Park Lane and to list its facilities including dining room, sleeping accommodation, reading and writing rooms, smoke room and coffee room with television. A close relationship with the club would continue for more than twenty years until its closure.]

'*Your committee's suggestion is that there should be two categories of membership within The Battle of Britain Fighter Association i.e. Full*

Membership and Associate Membership. Full membership would be for those who wish to give the Association the maximum support especially those living in London or who visit London from time to time. Associate membership is intended for those who never come to London and our overseas members. The proposed annual subscription for full members would be 12s.6d per head of which 10s.6d. would be the membership fee to be paid to the Reserves Club. The remaining 2s.0d. would cover administrative running costs such as the provision of wreaths, stationery, stamps, etc. [this compared with a subscription of 5s.0d. which had previously been agreed. The subscription now proposed for Associate members – a category later abolished – was 2s.0d.]

Later in the newsletter:-

'*Now that we are a going concern I have written officially to our President, Vice President and ex officio Vice Presidents inviting them to take up their respective duties forthwith. They have all accepted.*

    President – Lord Dowding, G.C.B., G.C.V.O.,C.M.G.

    Life Vice-President – Air Chief Marshal Sir Keith Park, G.C.B., K.B.E., M.C., D.F.C., D.C.L.

    Ex Officio Vice Presidents – The Chief of the Air Staff Sir Dermot Boyle, G.C.B., K.C.V.O, K.B.E, A.F.C.

    The Commander-in-Chief, Fighter Command Sir Thomas Pike, K.C.B., C.B.E., D.F.C.'

The newsletter went on to exhort members to support the Association's activities. There was an indication that the committee was '*anxious to extend the painstaking research carried out by Flight Lieutenant Holloway until every pilot or member of aircrew, still surviving and qualified to wear the Battle of Britain Clasp, is included in the list to be forwarded to you.*'

At this point in the BBFA's affairs the Secretary was Squadron Leader Don Higgin, an officer who had not qualified for the Battle of Britain Clasp.

Newsletter No 2, dated April 13 1959 was signed, as Chairman, by Air Vice-Marshal John Worrall. In fact, using his well-known nickname, he signed as 'Baron Worrall'.

He noted that:

'As many will already know, Air Commodore S C Widdows handed over the chairmanship on his recent retirement [from the RAF]. *The Annual General Meeting gave a unanimous Vote of Thanks for his valuable services in getting the Association reconstituted on a firm and satisfactory basis. We offer him congratulations on his appointment as a Companion of the Most Honourable Order of the Bath (C.B.) and wish him all good fortune in his retirement.*

'Also under change has been the Hon. Secretary. Squadron Leader Don Higgin, whose able endeavours contributed so much to the success of the gathering last September, has likewise retired. Our good wishes go with him too. The Secretaryship now passes to Wing Commander R.W. Oxspring, whose arrival at the Air Ministry coincided with his offering to take over (after a slight hesitancy when he suddenly remembered his 1369!).'

[Form 1369 was the means by which the annual confidential report on RAF officers was recorded. It was generally considered that having 'secondary duties' noted, for example acting as mess secretary, was good for career prospects. The present secretary of the BBFA, Patrick Tootal, recalls that his first 'secondary duty' was as officer in charge of F540/1, the ops record book on No 24 Squadron. On that basis Bobby Oxspring should perhaps have been pleased at his new appointment.]

Oxspring appears to have found that dealing with Flight Lieutenant Holloway could sometimes have its difficulties. Despite the marvellous work that Holloway had carried out in compiling the list of battle participants and the glowing tributes paid to him, he, of course, had the rest of his life to lead.

Material in the BBFA files shows that he was frequently asked to pass judgement on the credentials of those claiming entitlement to the clasp, not least when they visited Gieves the tailor to purchase a BBFA tie. Sometimes John Holloway's responses were not as swift as the BBFA officers hoped for.

A letter from Bobby Oxspring to John Holloway dated July 14 1959 and sent to his home in West Ealing is a good example:

'*Dear Holloway*

Thank you for your letter of 12th July [This date appears to have been altered in ink to 6 July.]

'*Medworth and Munn will be sent the circulars for this year's Reunion when they are distributed early next month.*

'*I have informed Gieves by 'phone that they are bona fide.*

'Would you please send me some sort of up-to-date list of chaps. I am continually being asked questions and would like some sort of guide. Air Vice-Marshal Worrall and Gieves are both in the same boat.
'Yours sincerely'

Flight Lieutenant Medworth had flown at least 14 operational sorties in the battle as a Sergeant Air Gunner with No 25 Squadron at North Weald.

Squadron Leader Munn was a pilot in the battle, flying as a Flight Sergeant with No 29 Squadron. He was awarded the DFM in 1941.

From the earliest days, the Association tie was considered very important. The newsletter dated 20 July 1960 gave notice of that year's reunion at Bentley Priory. The plan was that there would be a dinner at Bentley Priory but if more than 150 applications to attend were received, this would be reduced to a buffet. Dress was to be lounge suits and Baron Worrall demanded of members, 'Please wear your Battle of Britain Tie (obtainable from Gieves, 27, Old Bond Street, W.1. 21/9d each post paid).' Stanmore Park offered 'limited dormitory accommodation'.

A previous appeal for wartime photographs of members was repeated to add to a collection which the Association wished to create.

The 1960 AGM appointed Group Captain Johnnie Hill to the committee to address publicity matters. It was felt that air attachés overseas should be enlisted to publicise the fact that the Association wished to recruit clasp holders as members, though it was accepted that this would not be effective behind the Iron Curtain.

At the reunion, a message from the former Prime Minister was read:

'On the twentieth anniversary of the Battle of Britain I send you all my good wishes and my thoughts of the ever-memorable autumn of 1940, in which the Royal Air Force saved our country.
Winston S. Churchill'

The Association responded with a telegram:

'Warm greetings and sincere thoughts on the occasion of the reunion of the Battle of Britain Fighter Association from all members. We deeply appreciate your personal message.'

Cables were also sent to Sir Keith Park and 'Sailor' Malan (South African CO of No 74 Squadron in 1940, who was in poor health) reading, *'Greetings and best wishes from all at reunion of Battle of Britain Fighter Association.'*

At this stage the Association committee consisted of: Air Commodore A.R.D. MacDonell (Chairman), who was serving as Director of Works Study at the Air Ministry, Group Captain C.F. Gray (Secretary), Group Captain J.W. White (both at the Air Ministry), Group Captain T.P. Gleave, retired from the RAF, but employed in the Cabinet Office (Historical Section), Wing Commander R.F.T. Doe, serving at HQ Fighter Command, Bentley Priory, Group Captain John Cunningham whose mail was sent to the de Havilland Aircraft Co at Hatfield, Group Captain J.H. Hill, c/o National Overseas & Grindleys Bank Ltd, 54 Parliament Street, SW1 and Howard Duart who was living in Banstead, Surrey.

A difficulty continued to be the lack of anything approaching a full list of those entitled to membership – not least one that could easily be consulted by each member of the committee. Therefore Howard Duart found himself in the position of querying the status of Group Captain John Ellis, whom he did not know. Group Captain Ellis had remitted a payment. This issue was easily resolved. John Ellis had commanded No 610 Squadron in the battle.

More tricky was an apparent attempt from the membership to admit Air Chief Marshal Sir Basil Embry to the Association. This was not put forward on the basis of his hospitality when heading Fighter Command, but rather because it was suggested that he had flown qualifying sorties.

Embry (1902–1977) had an enormous reputation in the RAF, both for his achievements and for his distinctive manner which could both charm and intimidate. He had spent his service career showing a determination, as one of his contemporaries put it, 'to march towards the sound of the guns'. In 1960 Embry had been retired from the RAF for four years and was living in Australia.

Twenty years earlier Basil Embry had been in command of No 107 Squadron operating Blenheims in Bomber Command. In late May 1940 he was already highly decorated and about to relinquish his command to be promoted to Group Captain and command of a station. On a sortie against advancing German troops in France, Embry's Blenheim was shot down and he was one of two members of the crew taken prisoner. His NCO Air Gunner was killed. Embry quickly escaped from a column of prisoners and eventually regained England via Spain and Gibraltar.

After two months of recovery Embry had brief spells at HQ No 6 Group and then on the staff at Bentley Priory. He then went to Rochford by the end of October to lead night fighting operations from there.

According to Basil Embry himself in his autobiography *Mission Completed* he commanded a 'Nightfighter Wing' at Rochford comprising No 151 Squadron with Hurricanes and No 264 Squadron (Defiants), although *RAF Squadrons* (Jefford) gives the locations of these units at the time as Digby and Kirton-in-Lindsey respectively. The claim made on behalf of Embry was that he had flown more than one qualifying sortie in Beaufighters of No 25 Squadron, then at Debden. In December Embry took command of the Wittering sector.

Whatever the merits of the claim made on behalf of Embry, the man himself made it clear that he did not wish the matter to be pursued. To this day Embry does not feature on the official lists of Battle of Britain airmen.

This was far from being the only membership matter for discussion. A list was prepared in July 1960 of members who had been admitted, but should now be deleted because they did not qualify. At this stage the Association was in touch with about 600 personnel considered to qualify for membership.

The debate over entitlement to membership at that time is illustrated by a letter sent on 29 June 1960 by Group Captain Gray, to Captain J.S. Shorthouse, DFC, c/o Tasman Empire Airways in Auckland, New Zealand. Gray wrote:

'*I have had a letter from Wing Commander J.R.C. Young, dated 14th May 1960 stating that he had recently met you in Sydney, that you were a claimant to the Battle of Britain Clasp and were not yet a member of the Battle of Britain Fighter Association.*

'*Young also told me that you were in the PRU* [Photographic Reconnaissance Unit] *at Heston under Geoffrey Tuttle from July to October or November of 1940.*

'*I have checked this information with our expert* [Holloway] *who tells me that you are not on our Master List and that the PRU is not a qualifying unit. It would therefore appear that you are not eligible for membership of the Association. However, I will state that the qualification for membership is eligibility to wear the Battle of Britain Clasp to the 1939–45 Star. If you are eligible for this decoration I should be glad if you would provide me with further details, such as Service Number, war time rank, squadron number and details of operational sorties flown.*'

In this era groupings of clasp holders based overseas were being established. An Australian division of the BBFA was formally operating, with Squadron Leader John Cock as secretary. Though the word 'division' was later dropped, a loose organization of Australian residents in membership of the association continued into the 21st century.

In South Africa there was a nascent division, with four participants who were members of the BBFA, Group Captain A.D. Farquar, Squadron Leader J.R.A. Bailey, Group Captain A.G. Malan and Flight Lieutenant R.E. Jones. In addition, a number of potential members were listed: Wing Commander A.J.M. Aldwincle, Wing Commander M.N. Crossley, Flight Lieutenant A.D. Cumbers, Squadron Leader L.W. Graham, Flying Officer I.B.D.E. Hay, Group Captain Z. Krasnodebski, Squadron Leader A.G. Lewis (for whom no address was available), Flight Lieutenant A. O'Connell, Flight Lieutenant G.C.C. Palliser and Flight Lieutenant A.V. Watkinson.

Members also organised themselves to a greater or lesser extent in other countries. Often a key objective was to arrange visits to Britain at the time of each year's commemorations of the battle.

In 1965 for example a contingent of Canadian veterans visited Britain for the 25th anniversary commemorations and twenty-one clasp holders living in Australia and New Zealand were flown to the UK by RAF Transport Command. At that stage there had been campaigning by the association for several years to achieve the presence of Czechoslovak or Polish veterans of the battle, despite the barrier of the 'Iron Curtain' across Europe.

In the 25th anniversary year success was achieved and a warm welcome to the Association's AGM was given to Ottokar ('Otto') Hruby, recently in prison in Czechoslovakia. Hruby had served in the Czech Air Force from 1932 and had escaped, when the Germans arrived, to join the French Foreign Legion and, after the outbreak of war, the French Air Force. After the fall of France he had reached Liverpool from Algeria and enlisted in the RAFVR. Otto Hruby flew Hurricanes with No 111 Squadron in the Battle of Britain and was later awarded the DFC. He returned to Czechoslovakia at the end of the war and died in 1993.

There was also a notable attendee from Eastern Europe in 1966 when Air Commodore MacDonell was able to welcome Air Marshal Karel Janousek, who had been a key figure in establishing the Czech contribution to the RAF during the war.

A major change in the way the Association was run occurred at the AGM held on 15 September 1964 at Bentley Priory, as the following extract from the minutes shows:

Office of Chairman
'*Gp Capt Gleave advised the meeting that Air Cdre MacDonell was retiring from the RAF in November 1964 and that consideration must be given to a successor. In the past it had been considered advisable to appoint a senior officer who was serving at the Air Ministry. However, whilst this had advantages, there were certain drawbacks, not the least being the number of changes that had taken place. As an example he pointed out that prior to the present Chairman there had been three changes in a relatively short space of time. As regards the advantages the Chairman said these were in the main associated with the provision of clerical and office services. The meeting was asked to consider this last point and the desirability of the Association now standing on its own feet as regards these facilities; this of course would cost money.*

'*Lord Dowding was then asked if he would like to comment at this stage. The President stated that in his opinion the advantages of having a serving officer at AM* [Air Ministry] *as chairman had been overestimated when the turbulence involved was taken into consideration. He continued by paying a personal tribute to Air Cdre MacDonell and said that the Battle of Britain Fighter Association owed a great deal to him for the amount of work that he had undertaken on the Association's behalf, and said that he would wholeheartedly support his re-election. He concluded by saying that it would be worthwhile approaching the MOD to ask if the same facilities could be made available to Air Cdre MacDonell after his retirement as had been previously provided.*

'*The Chairman* [Group Captain Gleave acting in that capacity] *then put to the meeting the question of Air Cdre MacDonell's re-election as Chairman it having been previously confirmed by the Chairman that the Air Cdre would be agreeable to such a move. The suggestion was enthusiastically received and was accepted unanimously.*
'*Proposed by Lord Dowding*
'*Seconded by Wg Cdr M H Constable-Maxwell*

Early in 1965 came the death of Sir Winston Churchill. The BBFA was consulted on the way in which The Few should be represented at the State Funeral. Eventually the Air Force Department decided that, marching in the procession, there would be a contingent of thirteen pilots from the battle who were still serving. Air Commodore Deere led Group Captains Bartlett, Berry, Brothers, Brunner, Dutton, Ellacombe, Haine, Ingle, Oxspring, Sheen, Wootten and Wright. The Association sent a message of sympathy to Lady Churchill.

In the same year the 25th anniversary of the battle occupied much time and thought. Members were given a list of commemorative events that they could attend. As well as the Westminster Abbey service on Sunday, 19 September and a Guildhall reception the following day, these were:

- Wednesday, 15 September– BBFA AGM and annual dinner, at HQ Fighter Command, Bentley Priory
- Friday, 17 September– Visit to RAF Wattisham
- Saturday, 18 September– Battle of Britain Open Day at RAF Biggin Hill
- Wednesday, 22 September – Visit to British Aircraft Corporation factory at Weybridge
- Thursday, 23 September – Visit to Double Your Money television show at the Wembley studios

Whether any member had the stamina to complete the set from the conviviality of the AGM and annual dinner, through to the mock solemnity of TV host Hughie Green at Wembley is not recorded.

A significant event in 1967 was the issue to a very limited number of people of 'A Nominal Roll of Pilots and Aircrew who fought in the Battle of Britain – 10th July to 31st October 1940'. The distribution list was: Lord Dowding, Chief of the Air Staff, Chairman, Honorary Secretary, Honorary Treasurer and two committee members of the BBFA, General Secretary Royal Air Forces Association, RAF Benevolent Fund (Wing Commander Westmacott) and Air Historical Branch. This list was signed by Wing Commander Hopkin as BBFA Secretary and dated in ink, 17/1/67.

Columns on each page gave the rank of individuals in 1940 and in 1961, service number airman, service number officer, date commissioned, name, pilot or aircrew, nationality, decorations, squadrons served with in the battle, nicknames, current address or date killed and address of next of kin.

Recipients were enjoined: *'In view of the private addresses given it is requested that you will treat confidentially this nominal roll of pilots and aircrew who fought in the Battle of Britain.'*

The 1968 AGM considered an approach from the German *Stern* magazine to photograph British and German pilots from the battle together. This was described as 'controversial' in a subsequent newsletter and the discussion on the matter as 'full-blooded'. The idea was rejected.

In 1969 the events of 1940 were very much in the public eye with the world premiere, on 15 September that year, of the film *Battle of Britain*. To fit in with the premiere, the AGM and reunion of the Fighter Association was held on 14 September. The importance attached to the film had been indicated the previous year when the AGM had been addressed by member and adviser to the film, 'Ginger' Lacey and leading personnel involved in the making of the movie were given the privilege of being invited to the reunion.

Members received the following information in a newsletter dated August 1969:

'Those of you who have asked to attend the World Premiere in London, with or without partner, will have received from United Artists their formal invitation. This will now be followed by admission tickets bearing your seat numbers, dress instructions and timing.

'For the London Premiere it will be as well to be at the Dominion Theatre by 19.30 hours on the evening of Monday September 15th. There will be a very large number of guests to be received before the performance begins.

'Your committee discussed the question of dress for the ladies and, bearing in mind that serving officers will be in Mess Kit and that the Lord Mayor and Lady Mayoress will be attending the Guildhall Reception which follows the Premiere, we thought that long evening dress would be appropriate for the occasion.

'On the subject of seating in the Dominion Theatre, it is Lord Dowding's wish that he should have his 'Chicks' seated round him for the London Premiere. The centre stalls have, therefore, been reserved for the Battle of Britain Fighter Association members and their ladies, with a place of honour amidst them for our President and Lady Dowding.

'For those of you who have elected to attend the premiere in your region, i.e. at Nottingham, Leeds, Newcastle, Edinburgh, Glasgow, Liverpool, Manchester, Birmingham, Cardiff, Belfast and Sheffield on the 15th

September, the Area Secretaries of the Royal Air Forces Association will be contacting all concerned. Should those of you who have stated your intention to attend have any queries or do not receive instructions by the end of the month they should contact Mr Reginald Boak, General Secretary, Royal Air Forces Association, 43 Grove Park Road, Chiswick, London W4.'

After further administrative information, the newsletter mentioned that year's Service of Thanksgiving in Westminster Abbey on 21 September, before giving details of a Royal Gala Performance of *Battle of Britain* on Monday, 20 October, also at the Dominion Theatre. This was to be attended by Her Majesty the Queen and other members of the Royal Family, the date having been selected as that, *'most suitable to Her Majesty on her return from Scotland'*.

It was recorded that: *'The Queen's Colour Squadron will line the approach to the theatre and the Central Band of the RAF will march from Whitehall and the RAF trumpeters will sound the fanfare prior to the commencement of the film.'* Attending the Royal occasion would be, *'a small representative body of the Association ... who were selected by ballot from all the members.'* There were plans, on the same date, for premieres in Australia, New Zealand, Canada and South Africa.

The proceeds of the Royal Gala Performance and the Premieres outside London were to go to the Royal Air Forces Association and the Royal Air Force Benevolent Fund. While the World Premiere was 'invitation only', the money raised by the sale of programmes would also go to the two charities.

A major and very sad event in the history of the Association occurred not long after these happy occasions, as recorded in the archives:

Extract From Battle of Britain Fighter Association News Letter No 24, August 1970

From: Air Commodore A.R.D MacDonell CB DFC RAF (Ret'd)

'You will forgive me if this Newsletter is short and possibly uninspired.

'Our reunion next month will fall on 30th anniversary of the Battle of Britain: It will also be the first Reunion since our President's death. While his going has deprived us all of something much more personal than the loss of our one-time Commander-in-Chief and our Association's President the fact that he lived to see the launching of the great film and celebrations that I wrote about in my last Newsletter must hearten us.

'Those, like me, privileged to be close at hand during these stirring days last autumn, will bear witness to Stuffy's delight and immense happiness at the success of the film.

'Tom Gleave and I were invited by the family to attend the very moving and simple cremation ceremony just outside Tunbridge Wells on February 18th. We were present on the following morning when the ashes were taken into Westminster Abbey to rest there before the Memorial Service.

The Memorial Service
'The Memorial Service to our President was held at 12 noon on Thursday 12th March in Westminster Abbey.

'The Air Force Department asked me to guide them in the selection of an escort of ex-Battle of Britain pilots to process behind the casket at the beginning of the Service. There were to be sixteen of us. I chose Tom Gleave to bear the casket containing the ashes. I did my best to choose the fifteen that followed from as representative a cross-section as possible.

'The family invited me to accompany the small private procession to the RAF Memorial Chapel for the internment of the casket. In this way I represented you in company with Sir John Grandy and Lord Winterbottom.

'The ceremony of the Service was dignified and deeply moving; the address read by Denis Healey was excellent and the music was of the very high standard we have grown to expect from the Westminster choir.

[The Rt Hon Denis Healey, later Lord Healey, was Secretary of State for Defence at the time of the memorial service. Lord Winterbottom was a businessman and politician whose allegiance moved between various parties. At this time he was Parliamentary Under Secretary of State, RAF at the Ministry of Defence. He had served in the Royal Horse Guards in the Second World War.]

In 1971 the practice began of BBFA members paying tribute at Lord Dowding's grave in Westminster Abbey before each annual Battle of Britain service. On the first occasion the wreath was laid by the 2nd Lord Dowding, son of the former Commander in Chief, who, as Flying Officer Derek Dowding, had flown Spitfires in No 74 Squadron, under his father's command, in the Battle of Britain.

While the Association has always worked closely with the major RAF charities, welfare has unsurprisingly become an increasing issue over the years.

A sign of this in 1972 came with a newsletter intimation that funds were available to provide at least one form of assistance.

Don MacDonell wrote:

> *'I should I think bring up the hardy annual of how to make contact with our members whose financial circumstances make it impossible for them to meet the costs of travelling to London for our Reunion.*
>
> *'I cannot ask those who are in this position to write to me, for I know that pride makes this well nigh impossible. But we do have a certain amount of cash ... and, if anyone knows of a member who could, and would, accept a subsidised journey, if only on a once and for all basis, please let Howard Duart, who holds the purse strings, know.'*

Amongst those attending the ceremonies that year was Josef Koukal who had flown as a sergeant with No 310 Squadron in the battle. He had been shot down on 7 September 1940 and badly injured and burned. It was as a guest of the Guinea Pig Club that Koukal was allowed to come to England by the Czech authorities. He had previously spent fourteen years living in one room, with no water, along with his wife and two sons. During his stay Koukal laid a wreath at the RAF Memorial in tribute to all the Czechs who had served in the RAF. He also met the widow of the farmer on the Isle of Sheppey who had ripped off his burning clothes in 1940. He was presented with a piece of the wreckage from his aircraft.

Air Chief Marshal Sir Keith Park accepted an invitation to become President of the Association in succession to Lord Dowding. When Sir Keith died in 1975 there was much debate on who, if anyone, should succeed him and eventually the post was left in abeyance.

The Association was still a large and active body. It was recorded in 1977 that there were about 600 members receiving newsletters and 110 of them were present at the AGM at Bentley Priory in September that year.

The meeting was informed that Flight Lieutenant Howard Duart wished to stand down as Secretary and Treasurer after twenty years in post. His elected successor from 1978 was Wing Commander Pat Hancock who would also serve in those key roles for many years. Hancock, a genial man with the clipped tone and straight to the point approach, that told of his military background, continued at least one habit of Howard Duart's. When he was approached by researchers he would pass on their stamped letters to appropriate members, provided that a stamped addressed envelope was included. Later secretaries maintained the practice, ensuring the survival of an enormous body of information and anecdote relating to the battle.

It was in 1977, the year of the Queen's Silver Jubilee, that Her Majesty Queen Elizabeth the Queen Mother agreed to become Patron of the Association. Even in the late seventies, Sir Christopher Foxley-Norris, as chairman from 1978, was commenting on the difficulties of continuity of such an exclusive body, with a qualification for membership relating only to a short period in the year 1940. With that circumstance it was inevitable that there would come a point when the Association no longer existed in its traditional form and consideration should be given as to how its ethos was to be kept going, though at the time the matter was far from urgent.

In 1982 the Association AGM returned to Bentley Priory after three years with RAF West Drayton as an excellent host venue. The reason for the temporary move had been the major fire causing much damage at Bentley Priory on 21 June 1979. Despite the hospitality offered at West Drayton, there was evidently great delight at returning to the spiritual home of the Association.

For some years in the 1980s, the Association was much concerned with fund raising and seeking a site and the appropriate permissions for a statue of Lord Dowding in central London. An early proponent of this project was Flight Lieutenant Roger Hall who had been a Spitfire pilot with No 152 Squadron in the Battle of Britain. A sub-committee dealing with the project was headed by Wing Commander Peter Parrott who had flown Hurricanes with No 145 Squadron. As was sometimes the case in the days when the Association had a large membership, the sub-committee had to consider many, sometimes opposing, ideas on the subject from members. The wish for a statue of Dowding was eventually fulfilled at St Clement Danes church as detailed in the chapter on memorials.

As the decade wore on, plans for the 50th anniversary of the battle in 1990 became a significant matter for discussion. For years the Association had been raising funds to bring overseas members to reunions under the title of 'Operation Homecoming'. Efforts were re-doubled as 1990 approached and a very large turnout was secured for events in that year. At the AGM and reunion 170 members living in the UK were present and a further 126 had travelled from around the world, including the USA, Australia, South Africa, Canada, New Zealand, France, Spain, Poland, Czechoslovakia and Cyprus.

A number had been taken ill on their way to the events including Sir Ronald Lees and Don Kingaby. The meeting remembered Jack Mann, at that time held as a hostage in Lebanon.

In the mid nineties the long-term future of the Association was again on the agenda. A major step came in 1995 when Malcolm Smith became the first non-clasp holder to be appointed secretary and treasurer, replacing Pat Hancock who was in poor health.

Malcolm Smith had served in the Army and was well known to Association members through his commemorative activities and writing. However, as he would later recall, he was given an intense grilling, led by Sir Christopher Foxley-Norris, before he was appointed to the roles. His successor in 2005, Group Captain Patrick Tootal, had the advantage of having been an RAF pilot, albeit long after the Second World War.

For many of the members, attending at least some of the 60th anniversary events in 2000 became a target as the turn of the century approached. Plenty made it triumphantly. Around seventy reached the Kent coast in July 2000 to attend a lunch in Dover, laid on by the council and the annual Memorial Day at the National Memorial to The Few at Capel-le-Ferne. At the Dover lunch, the significant group of veterans of No 501 Squadron asked for their own table. Amongst those present who had served on the squadron was 'Skalski', Squadron Leader Stanislaw Skalski, who later in the war in the Western Desert, led the Polish unit known as 'Skalski's Circus'. He had travelled from Poland for the events.

As the majority of the veterans of the battle headed towards and passed into their 90s, the issue became firmly not just the provision of assistance from younger people, but the existence itself of the Association. In addition leading figures were departing. Her Majesty Queen Elizabeth the Queen Mother died in 2002 and His Royal Highness the Prince of Wales agreed to become Patron. For a number of years he would offer hospitality to the members each summer, until the number able to take part became very small.

Sir Christopher Foxley-Norris died in 2003 and Air Commodore Peter Brothers became chairman. Following the passing of 'Pete' Brothers in 2008, Wing Commander Bob Foster was appointed chairman, serving until his death in 2014.

Over a considerable number of years informal discussions took place with the Battle of Britain Memorial Trust. These were aided by the fact that Patrick Tootal was secretary of both bodies. It became clear from these discussions that the Memorial Trust was the natural successor organization, to be charged with continuing the ethos of the BBFA after the veterans of the battle had departed the scene.

Patrick Tootal's summary of the situation, writing in 2014, was:

'There was a close relationship between Clive Hunting and Geoffrey Page [Clasp holder and founder of the Trust] when the Trust was formed. Christopher Foxley-Norris was President of the Trust and Clive was the Chairman and a great benefactor. Christopher Foxley-Norris was also Chairman of the Fighter Association. It was Air Chief Marshal Foxley–Norris who issued a three line whip for BBFA members to turn out for Memorial Day at Capel-le-Ferne. With Malcolm Smith's incapacitation his wife Joyce recommended to Pete Brothers, by then Chairman of the BBFA, that I take over in that body.'

The links between the Association and Trust took a formal step forward at the BBFA AGM held at the RAF Club on 14 September 2013 when the following resolution was passed:

'That the Committee of The Association be authorised to take all such action as it considers appropriate to seek to agree terms for, and (subject to such terms being satisfactory to the committee and to the fulfillment of any applicable conditions) then to implement, a transfer to the Battle of Britain Memorial Trust whether in its present or any reconstituted form ("the Trust") of the undertaking of The Association with a view to the activities of the Association being carried on following such transfer by the Trust in a manner consistent with objects from time to time of the Trust.'

Nonetheless, as the 75th anniversary of the Battle of Britain approached, the BBFA remained very active and running its own affairs. In the summer of 2014 there were still thirty-eight clasp holders in membership.

Chapter Four

Westminster Abbey and the Roll of Honour

S ome of the most important letters illustrating the early involvement of Westminster Abbey in the listing of The Few and the commemoration of the Battle of Britain are quoted in this chapter.

Captain Bruce Ingram was a wealthy and patriotic man with a particular determination that the names of The Few should be recorded for all time. He wrote to Sir Archibald Sinclair, Secretary of State for Air, in July 1942, offering to pay for the preparation of a scroll containing the names for presentation to Westminster Abbey. While the initiative was welcome at the Air Ministry, the problem was immediately apparent that would run as a theme down the years. Who should be on the list? In addition, what practical prospects were there of compiling an acceptable list in wartime?

The official view transmitted to Ingram was that the scroll should contain the names of those serving in Fighter Command who had been killed in battle. Ingram appealed again to Sinclair, in a letter on 1 September 1942, saying that his opinion was that the scroll should contain, *'the names of the pilots of the fighter planes that went into the air to defend Britain, as it is obvious that one who came through the ordeal was just as great a hero as one who was killed in the action.'*

To the Air Ministry it still seemed impossible, in wartime at least, to ensure that everybody was covered, including those who might have been attached from one squadron to another or been kept out of the fighting through illness. The correspondence also indicated that at this point it was considered that some judgement might need to be made on the performance of participants. It seems to have been felt that it might be appropriate to exclude any who had not had the will to continue.

Civil service language unsurprisingly crept into the drafting of Sinclair's reply that referred to finding a solution which, amongst other things, was 'suitable' and 'uncontroversial'. Sinclair's opinion was that the scroll should feature the names of fighter pilots and air gunners who had been lost. Ingram accepted this partial rebuff to his ambition with regret, while hoping that another look might be taken at the matter after the war.

A list to meet the Air Ministry requirement was compiled in Fighter Command in late 1942 and early 1943 and signed off as accurate by Air Marshal Sir Trafford Leigh-Mallory, Air Officer Commanding. This list covers the period 8 August to 31 October 1940 and appears at Appendix 1. The scroll went ahead with the work being carried out by the outstanding calligrapher Daisy Alcock.

Not so long after Bruce Ingram's intervention another correspondent raised the matter of the Battle of Britain with the Dean of Westminster. On 8 March 1943 from Duni House, Minsterworth, Gloucester, N.P.W. Viner-Brady, a solicitor, began his letter:

> '*Dear Mr Dean*
>
> '*I venture to recall myself to you. You may remember that Mr Rushforth and I, as Executors of the late Mr H.C. Embleton, had the pleasure of meeting you at Methley in connection with the repairs to Methley Church and the Memorial Window and Screen to be placed there to his Memory.*
> [Dean de Labilliere had been Rector of Methley, near Leeds.]
>
> '*I am venturing to write to you with a suggestion which if it meets with your approval could only be carried out with the sanction of yourself as Dean of Westminster. We have the Tomb of The Unknown Warrior there. Should not there be a Memorial to Those Few to whom so many owe so much? We now know that those brave few not only saved Britain but probably the World.*'

Mr Viner-Brady went on to say that his inspiration was the 'Crécy Window' in Gloucester Cathedral, said to show the coats of arms of the Gloucestershire knights who had fought at the battle in 1346, part of the Hundred Years War. He proposed a window at Westminster Abbey that would display the names of all the participants in the Battle of Britain and the starting of a fund to achieve his objective.

Noel Philip Wentworth Viner-Brady did not live to see his ambition fulfilled. He died, aged 81, at Twickenham, Middlesex on 2 August 1945, after an illness 'most bravely and cheerfully borne'. He had been senior partner in Minet, Pering, Smith & Co, solicitors of Bedford Square, London. In addition he had held directorships of the Bedlington Coal Company, Chislet Colliery and the Wallsend and Hebburn Colliery Company. Viner-Brady's funeral took place at Minsterworth. His wife Elizabeth had died on 13 July 1945.

N.P.W Viner-Brady thus set rolling a most important ball in Battle of Britain commemoration, but his Gloucestershire inspiration was not soundly based. In 2013 Christopher Jeens, Archivist at Gloucester Cathedral Library, wrote:

> *'The 'Crecy window' is a name still sometimes given to Gloucester Cathedral's Great East Window. It seems to have started with Dean Spence in 1913 who believed that the heraldry displayed in it meant that it was intended to be a form of war memorial for those who fought at the Battle of Crécy in 1346. More modern scholarship has shown that the heraldry better matches those who fought with Edward III in his Scottish campaign and at the siege of Calais (both in that same year) and that it is a misunderstanding to think of it as a "war memorial" in the modern sense. However Dean Spence's view was probably generally accepted in the 1940s. At the time of its installation in what was then St Peter's Abbey it was the largest window in Western Europe.'*

The Dean of Westminster accepted the Viner-Brady proposal and chose a small chapel at the eastern end of Henry Vll's Lady Chapel. What would become the RAF Chapel had suffered bomb damage in September 1940 and a hole in the stonework was preserved and covered with glass. Fund raising proceeded for the stained glass window and for furnishings for the chapel, with the leading figure being Lord Trenchard, the former Chief of the Air Staff. Trenchard had initially shown some reluctance to become involved, at least partly because he doubted the wisdom of such a major tribute to one group of RAF heroes. However, he was persuaded and relented. Lord Dowding was on the committee which was established and so was Mr Viner-Brady.

An English walnut altar was designed by Professor A.E. Richardson with sculptured figures of King Arthur and St George, although an embroidered frontal usually covers them. The silver cross, candlesticks and rails were designed by J. Seymour Lindsay.

The Battle of Britain Memorial stained glass window, by Hugh Easton, features the badges of the fighter squadrons that took part in the battle, although the list was altered after the window was completed. The window is described thus by Westminster Abbey:

'*In four panels are shown visions which symbolise the Redemption. In one a Squadron Leader kneels before the Virgin Mary and the Christ Child. Below this she is represented in her sorrow with the dead Christ across her knees (a symbol of the sacrifice of the mothers and widows of those who died in the conflict). On the opposite side a panel shows a Sergeant pilot kneeling before the Crucifixion (a symbol of the sacrifice of the pilot himself). Lastly, above this, is the Resurrection seen by a Pilot Officer (representing the pilots' triumph). Seraphim, with six wings and with hands outstretched to paradise, are shown in the top row of the window. In the central section are the Royal Arms, the badge of the Fleet Air Arm and the badge and motto of the RAF "Per Ardua ad Astra" (Through struggle to the Stars) together with the furled flags of New Zealand, Canada, Australia, South Africa, Czechoslovakia, Poland, Belgium, and the United States of America. In two of the bottom panels are words from Shakespeare's Henry V "We few, we happy few, we band of brothers". Painted on the stonework below the glass are the names of six RAF war leaders (added in 1989). Trenchard and Dowding are buried in this chapel.*'

The Roll of Honour, donated by Bruce Ingram and produced by Daisy Alcock, contains the names of 1,497 aircrew killed or mortally wounded during the battle, of whom 449 were in Fighter Command (which the window specially commemorates), 732 in Bomber Command, 268 in Coastal Command, 14 in other RAF commands and 34 in the Fleet Air Arm.

Despite the role of the Air Ministry in deciding the names to be included on the roll, as well as in deciding the eligibility for the clasp, there is little correlation between the two, with inclusion on the roll being extended well beyond Fighter Command. Over the years this has added to confusion over eligibility for the Battle of Britain Clasp.

All the plans came together on the appropriately chosen 10 July 1947 when the Chapel and its contents were unveiled by King George VI. Relatives of those included on the Roll of Honour were invited to the occasion.

A difficulty quickly arose. Relatives of other aircrew began to claim that their loved one should have been included in the list and new research revealed more men with entitlement to be listed. These matters were considered and sometimes acted upon.

For example, the Roll was removed from public display from 13 December to 18 December 1947 so that the names of Flight Lieutenant H.W.A. Sheahan,

Pilot Officer C.J. Allsup and Sergeant S. Smith could be added. They had been the crew of a Hudson of No 220 Squadron, Coastal Command, which, on 1 August 1940, had flown into power lines and the bombs on board had exploded, killing the crew. Originally the three names had been left off the roll on the basis that the men had died in a flying accident, however, it was later accepted that they had been incorrectly omitted because they had been on an operational sortie at the time of their deaths. For some years at least Daisy Alcock was paid for the additional work generated by such decisions.

The practice of holding a Service of Thanksgiving in the Abbey for the victory gained in the Battle of Britain began in 1944 and has continued ever since. Each September members of The Few visit the RAF Chapel before the Thanksgiving service and pay tribute to Lord Dowding. His ashes and those of Lord Trenchard were interred beneath the chapel. The service always attracts a large attendance of people with RAF connections and others who wish to remember the part played by The Few in the country's defence.

Two of the letters in the story:

The *Illustrated London News*
1 New Oxford Street
London WC1
July 9 1942

'Dear Sir Archibald Sinclair

I am writing to ask if you can give me your co-operation in a scheme which I have had in view for some time past.

The Battle of Britain had such importance in the history of our Island that it is only comparable to the Defeat of the Spanish Armada and the Battle of Trafalgar.

Thus I think it quite necessary that a permanent record of the names of those who took an active part in the Battle should be preserved in a complete form, for the benefit of those who in the distant future have to write of the glory of Britain.

What I want to do is to have the full list of the participants in the actual battle of the skies during the most critical period, written by a leading calligraphist on gold leaf.

This I would have executed at my own expense and I would then present the scroll to, say the Dean of Westminster for preservation in the Abbey, or in any other body considered more suitable to keep the document.

I wish to make this gift not from any desire for personal publicity, for my name unless it is considered advisable need not appear, nor have I any intention of making use of the list in "The Illustrated London News", *unless you think such publication would be of national benefit.*

To get this scheme carried out, I should require your good offices in order to get the record complete.

Can you do this for me?

If so, I am sure that you would earn not only my gratitude but that of the many millions who realize the debt of gratitude we owe to those who kept the enemy from our shores.

Yours sincerely
Bruce Ingram

The *Illustrated London News*
Commonwealth House
1 New Oxford Street
London WC1

September 28 1943

The Rt Rev P.F.D de Labilliere DD MA
The Deanery
Westminster
London SW1

My dear Dr de Labilliere,

Last September I wrote to the Air Minister, Sir Archibald Sinclair, to suggest that an illuminated Scroll containing the names of all those who took an active part in the Battle of Britain would make a worthy record of those who were so instrumental in keeping this country free from invasion.

I said that I would be willing to defray the cost of this scroll and that it should be offered to you for permanent preservation.

It was, however, found impossible to supply the complete list of the participants living and dead, though Sir Archibald Sinclair was very appreciative of the proposal.

He then suggested that the scroll should take the form of a Roll of Honour containing the names of all those pilots and air gunners who lost their lives during the battle.

With this idea I concurred and the Roll of Honour is now being carried out by Miss Alcock, whose name was given to me as the best of our present day illustrators.

It will take the form of a volume bound in leather with a decoration specially designed, and contain about forty pages of the names written on vellum by the illustrator.

This book will take many months before it is completed, but I am writing to know if you will eventually accept it to be preserved in the Abbey Archives or in any other way you may think fit.

I may say here that it is not my wish that my name shall be connected with this gift; my only desire being that the names of those who gave their lives in a victory which, in its consequences, must forever rank with the Defeat of the Spanish Armada or the Battle of Trafalgar, shall be contained in a complete and, I trust, not inadequate record.

It would give me deep satisfaction to think that this record will rest in Westminster Abbey.

Hoping that you will be able to accede to this request,

I am, dear Dr de Labilliere,

Yours sincerely,

Bruce S. Ingram

(Editor)

Chapter Five

Remembering The Few

S ome examples of the ways in which the men who flew in the Battle of Britain are remembered.

The National Memorial to The Few, Capel-le-Ferne, Kent

Wing Commander Geoffrey Page, who conceived the idea of the memorial, was a Hurricane pilot with No 56 Squadron in 1940. On 12 August that year his aircraft was hit by return fire from German bombers he was attacking. Page was terribly burned before he managed to escape from the stricken aircraft.

He was rescued from the sea and became a patient of Archibald McIndoe at the Queen Victoria Hospital, East Grinstead. He would later recall his first contact at East Grinstead with the legendary McIndoe:

'The surgeon bent over my crippled hands, turning them over slowly as he examined the damage. Without raising his head he looked up over his glasses. "Long job, I'm afraid."

'Hesitantly I asked, "you'll have to operate?"

'This time the head went back and the dark eyes met mine firmly, "Yes many times I'm afraid. But you'll be alright in the end."'

'I believed him.'

Geoffrey Page did indeed recover and went back into action, before being injured again and returning to East Grinstead. (See also entry for 'The Guinea Pig Club' in this section.)

Many years later he conceived the idea of the National Memorial to The Few and he established the Battle of Britain Memorial Trust. There were various tribulations, but the site at Capel-le-Ferne was obtained. The sculptor Harry Gray created the memorial, an airman, with no indication of rank visible, seated in a three-bladed propeller and looking out over the Strait of Dover. On 9 July 1993, the official opening ceremony was performed by Her Majesty Queen Elizabeth the Queen Mother.

Geoffrey Page died in 2000, but the Memorial Trust has continued to develop the area of the memorial. In 2014 additional features included the Christopher Foxley-Norris Memorial Wall, on which are inscribed the names of the Allied airmen who took part in the battle and full-sized replicas of a Hurricane and a Spitfire from 1940. The Hurricane represents 'Little Willie' of No 56 Squadron, which Geoffrey Page was flying when he was shot down, while the Spitfire has the markings of an aircraft flown by the Supermarine test pilot, Flying Officer Jeffrey Quill, when he was attached to No 65 Squadron during the battle.

Each year on a Sunday in July a Memorial Day, supported by the RAF, is held at the memorial site.

In 2014 work was proceeding on a new visitor and education centre at the site, to be known as The Wing. It was intended that this major new feature would be in operation in time for the 75th anniversary commemorations of the battle.

The Trust has always been able to attract the participation of distinguished figures. In 2014 the Patron was HRH Prince Michael of Kent, the President was Air Chief Marshal Sir Michael Graydon, Chief of the Air Staff, 1992–1997. Two former Chiefs of the Air Staff, Air Chief Marshals Sir Peter Squire and Sir Stephen Dalton were Vice Presidents. The Chairman was Richard Hunting, Chairman of Hunting plc. A Life Vice President was Geoffrey Page's daughter Shelley Gubelmann. Two members of the Beaverbrook family were trustees.

The Hunting family has been a major supporter of the memorial throughout its existence. The company that bears the family name today is the successor to an enterprise founded in the 19th century and prominent in shipping and shipbroking from its early days.

Later Hunting moved into civil aviation, purchased the Percival Aircraft Company in 1944, launched Hunting Air Travel as a passenger carrier, worked with the Cayzer family to operate the Hunting-Clan airline and provided the Percival Provost and Hunting Jet Provost trainers for the RAF.

Today Hunting plc manufactures and distributes equipment for the extraction of oil and gas.

An individual pilot from the battle is specifically commemorated at the National Memorial. The footpath, Beazley Way, which leads down to the memorial from near the car and coach park is a tribute to Wing Commander John Beazley (1916–2011) who was Treasurer, and later a Life Vice President, of the Battle of Britain Memorial Trust.

John Beazley was 'Beazel' in 1940 when, as a Pilot Officer, he flew Hurricanes with No 249 Squadron. He had been a member of the Oxford University Air Squadron and then the RAFVR. He baled out of a burning Hurricane on 2 September and was wounded on 27 September.

He later recorded that he had some explaining to do when Air Chief Marshal Dowding visited the hospital ward in which John Beazley was recovering. The man who led Fighter Command in the battle was not impressed that Messerschmitt Bf 110s had twice been the cause of the downfall of the Hurricane pilot lying in bed before him. However, he seemed to accept 'Beazel's' plea in mitigation that there had been a lot of them about. John Beazley later flew into action from Malta.

Pilot Officer Herbert Case of No 72 Squadron, lost on 12 October 1940 is remembered on a display board at the National Memorial, his Spitfire having crashed on the other side of Capel-le-Ferne village. Following his death this letter was sent to his mother by the wife of an Army officer.

(Spelling and punctuation as in the original)
Dear Mrs Case

I have hesitated long before writing to send you some first hand news of your boys heroic end – a piece of the spitfire which I thought you might like to have.

I was staying at Capel Le Ferne, when the plane came down, two fields away from the bungalow, my husband and his platoon were on the spot instantly and his boys 70th Buffs had to do the guarding.

We had been watching the fight when 9 Messerschmiits swooped into two of ours. Everyone was terribly upset when the Spitfire was shot down. I have seldom seen my husband so affected, but he assured me that the boy must have been killed in the air before he crashed. I thought this knowledge might be of some small comfort to you in your tragic sorrow and pride, in the astonishing courage of these sons, whose deeds fill the world with admiration.

Forgive me for intruding, this is not meant like that, and requires no answer.'

Close to Capel-le-Ferne is the Kent Battle of Britain Museum on part of the former Hawkinge airfield and using some of the ex RAF buildings. The museum is run completely separately from the National Memorial but the two work together on marketing initiatives. There is a remarkable collection at Hawkinge of artefacts associated with the events of 1940, as well as photographs from the time, including many of the aircrew. Much refurbishment and modernisation was carried out over the winter of 2013/2014.

The Battle of Britain London Monument

The monument was the creation of the Battle of Britain Historical Society, an organization founded by Bill Bond. It stands on the Victoria Embankment, on the north side of the River Thames on land donated by Westminster Council, a short walk from the Houses of Parliament. It was unveiled in 2005 by HRH The Prince of Wales. The sculptor was Paul Day.

In the words of the Monument's website:

'The site is based on an existing panelled granite structure 25m long. This structure was originally designed as a smoke outlet for underground trains when they were powered by steam engines. It has been filled up and blocked for many years.

'A walkway has been cut obliquely through the middle of the existing structure and bronze reliefs, depicting aspects of the Battle in the air and the back-up on the ground, are positioned along either side. Bronze plaques holding in raised relief the names and ranks of the airmen who took part in the battle are mounted around the outside of the monument, the airmen's names being grouped under their respective countries.'

Close to the monument, at the head of Whitehall Stairs, is the Royal Air Force Memorial, in Portland stone and surmounted by a gilded eagle. The memorial was created on the initiative of the Royal Air Force Benevolent Fund in memory of airmen who died in the Great War. The eagle faces symbolically across the Thames toward France, where so many of those remembered were lost in that war.

The memorial was unveiled in 1923 by the then Prince of Wales, later King Edward Vlll. It survived bomb damage in the Second World War. Wreaths are frequently laid at the memorial, especially every year on Battle of Britain Sunday.

A website related to the Battle of Britain London Monument is maintained by Edward McManus at www.bbm.org.uk. As well as information about the monument, the website lists the airmen who took part in the battle, as shown on the monument, tells the stories of many of them, often with photographs and illustrates graves and memorials.

Typical of material on the website is this letter home, dated 15 August 1940, from Pilot Officer R.E. Jones, a pilot in No 605 Squadron, who survived the war and died in 1994. It describes his first contact with enemy raiders:

'I think I can give you some good news today. Yesterday our flight was "at available", which is to say we have to be on the camp and be able to get into the air within 15 minutes. At 11.45 a message came through that the whole squadron was to go up on patrol. Within 10 minutes we were climbing to 20,000 feet and heading out to sea. From there we were directed by the ground and heard that about 30 enemy aircraft were approaching. We cruised about and eventually found ourselves over Newcastle and the Tyne. I began to think we were on a wild goose chase because by this time we had been up for about one and three-quarter hours and we were being told to land at local aerodromes to refuel. There were only five of us left by that time; the others had drifted away. Suddenly over the leader's machine and about three miles away, I saw the biggest formation of enemy aeroplanes I have ever seen bigger than any I ever saw at Hendon air display and then another smaller formation behind them.

'Archie McKellar, my leader, decided to attack the big formation, so we turned and climbed into the sun. At that moment I ran out of petrol and by the time I had turned on to my reserve tank Archie was 200 years in front of me. We kept climbing until we were about 4,000 feet above the enemy and directly overhead. Then we turned on our backs and dived to attack.

'I found myself attacking two aircraft which were below each other and dead in my sights. As I came down I pressed my firing button and for the first time heard my guns go off I could see my bullets hitting the aircraft, when suddenly the starboard engine of one of the Heinkel's (111) exploded and left a long trail of black smoke.

'Almost immediately the port engine of the other machine caught fire and the last I saw of those two as I shot by at 400 m.p.h, they looked as if they would collide.

'*I pulled out of my dive and climbed up again well to one side of the formation and looked for Archie. I couldn't pick him out, so I decided to attack a lone aircraft which was a little way from the others – I went in from the side and as he went through my sights I followed him round.*

'*Suddenly his nose went straight up into the air, and then he toppled over and went straight into a spin. Two parachutes came out as the machine crashed toward the sea. I climbed up again and waited until I saw another straggler and then I went in again and pressed the button there was a roar and silence – I had run out of ammunition, so I dived towards the clouds and as I went I saw lots of bombs explode in the sea.*

'*My total bag for my first encounter is one Heinkel 111 shot down and two damaged. We lost two machines, but the pilots are safe; one came back to the aerodrome last night; the other is in hospital with concussion. My machine was not hit.*

'*We had a wizard champagne party in the mess last night. The whole of A Flight was unlucky, they didn't see a thing but our flight sent seven down and damaged six.*'

Bentley Priory Battle of Britain Trust

The Bentley Priory Battle of Britain Trust was established by Alan Curtis on behalf of the Battle of Britain Fighter Association, following the departure of the RAF from Bentley Priory in 2008.

The Trust's objects were laid down as:

'*To establish and maintain Bentley Priory, Stanmore in the London Borough of Harrow as a centre for education, information, training and teaching of the history of the Battle of Britain, aerospace history, aerospace technology and its future advancement;*

'*To use Bentley Priory as a permanent memorial to those who served in the Royal Air Force and in particular (but not exclusively) during the Battle of Britain in order to assist future generations in acknowledging and recognising the sacrifices made during the Battle of Britain to ensure freedom of Europe and the World.*'

In 2014 the Chairman of the Trustees was Air Chief Marshal Sir Brian Burridge. The Bentley Priory Museum was officially opened on 12 September 2013 by Their Royal Highnesses the Prince of Wales and the Duchess of Cornwall.

One man immediately enters the thoughts of many visitors to Bentley Priory. Air Chief Marshal Lord Dowding used 'Bentley Priory' as his geographical designation when he was made a peer and a bust of him was unveiled by the Royal couple as part of the museum's opening ceremony.

Talking to *Britain at War* magazine in 2013, Wing Commander Erica Ferguson who had overseen the development of the museum commented:

'We are telling the whole story of Bentley Priory, but, of course, the most crucial and well known element of the story is how Sir Hugh Dowding, as he then was, came here, planned the role of Fighter Command in the war that lay ahead and then implemented his plans, with what is justifiably called the Dowding system, at the centre of them, and played such a great part in saving Britain from what was likely to be a terrible fate.

'We know that not everybody agrees with the way Dowding did things and that others made massive contributions to the defence of Britain in 1940, but without Dowding perhaps the Germans would have arrived in London. He certainly dominates the atmosphere here at his old headquarters and seems to be keeping an eye on things through the bust. When I pass it I am sometimes tempted to say under my breath, "Are we doing it right, sir?".

Some of Dowding's towering reputation stems from the campaign in the spring of 1940, in which he played a leading role, to stop further Hurricane squadrons being drained away in the Battle of France.

Words from the letter, addressed to the Under Secretary of State for Air, (Harold Balfour MP), that he wrote on 16 May 1940 will be quoted in books on twentieth century history for many years hence.

The letter began:

'Sir

'I have the honour to refer to the very serious calls which have recently been made upon the Home Defence Fighter Units in an attempt to stem the German invasion on the Continent.

'2. I hope and believe that our Armies may yet be victorious in France and Belgium, but we have to face the possibility that they may be defeated.

'3. In this case I presume that there is no-one who will deny that England should fight on, even though the remainder of the Continent of Europe is dominated by the Germans.

'4. For this purpose it is necessary to retain some minimum fighter strength in this country and I must request that the Air Council will inform me what they consider this minimum strength to be, in order that I may make my dispositions accordingly.

'5. I would remind the Air Council that the last estimate which they made as to the forces necessary to defend this country was 52 Squadrons, and my strength has now been reduced to the equivalent of 36 Squadrons.'

St George's RAF Chapel of Remembrance, Biggin Hill

'The name has a homely sound, almost rustic, but there are squadrons of the Royal Air Force as proud of having fought from here as regiments in the Army are of having "Blenheim" and "Alamein" emblazoned on their colours.' From *RAF Biggin Hill* by Graham Wallace.

The idea that there should be a memorial chapel at Biggin Hill airfield developed in 1943, although there was already a station church.

The 2007 guidebook to the present chapel records that:

'RAF personnel thought it would be appropriate to have a memorial to the increasing number of aircrew who were being killed on operations from within the Biggin Hill sector, remembering especially those who had died in the Battle of Britain. Furthermore, there was a desire to commemorate that victory and to mark the destruction of the 1000th German aircraft by fighters from the Biggin Hill sector, which happened in June 1943.'

Three prefabricated huts were used to create the chapel and the building was dedicated on Battle of Britain Sunday on 19 September 1943. The Station Commander and Battle of Britain veteran, Group Captain 'Sailor' Malan, was present and it is believed that he read the lesson. Boards on each side of the altar listed those who had been killed while serving at the station.

This chapel was destroyed by fire in December 1946, possibly caused by an electrical fault. The padre, the Reverend Cecil King, encouraged by Winston Churchill, set about raising funds for a new chapel. He also made much effort to keep in touch with the families of service personnel who had been killed, including through newsletters.

The foundation stone was laid on a new site by Lord Dowding in July 1951 and the building was dedicated by the Bishop of Rochester in November that year. Service chapels are often dedicated, rather than consecrated as in theory they are part of temporary encampments and may have other uses in the future. The first chaplain at the new chapel was the Reverend Vivian Symons, vicar of Biggin Hill.

Today's visitor to the chapel finds fine stained glass windows, the work of Hugh Easton, who was also responsible for the memorial window at Westminster Abbey. There are also many artefacts associated with Biggin Hill's wartime role.

One of these is the book of remembrance, which contains the names of 450 airmen from twelve countries who gave their lives. The book was compiled by Hugh Jay in memory of his brother-in-law, Sub Lieutenant Geoffrey Gordon Robson Bulmer RN who was attached to No 32 Squadron in Fighter Command during the Battle of Britain and who was killed in action on 20 July 1940. It took Mr Jay three years to complete the book.

On 6 October 1963 a memorial service was held in the chapel for Group Captain 'Sailor' Malan who had died in South Africa on 17 September that year. The service was conducted by the Reverend J.N. Wilson who had been the station chaplain in 1940 and the address was given by the Reverend Cecil King. Lord Dowding was present. The Commandant at Biggin Hill at the time was Air Commodore Bobby Deacon Elliott who, as Pilot Officer Elliott, had fought in 1940 with No 72 Squadron. Malan had been given a civic funeral by the South African city of Kimberley.

Outside the chapel are gate guardians dedicated in 2010 to replace earlier guardians which were in a poor state of repair. The aircraft now represented are Hurricane P 2921 of No 32 Squadron, flown by Flight Lieutenant 'Pete' Brothers during the Battle of Britain and Spitfire K 9998 of No 92 Squadron, flown by Pilot Officer Geoffrey 'Boy' Wellum. The cost of them was raised by the Friends of the Chapel.

In 2014 St George's Chapel was expected to be open to visitors on every day of the year between at least 11am and 4pm, except for Christmas Day, when it would only open for a service. During the rest of the year services would be held regularly. Although the RAF had long departed from Biggin Hill, at that time the Chapel remained within the remit of the RAF chaplaincy at Northolt.

In late 2014 the Ministry of Defence announced its intention to dispose of the chapel by March 2016.

On 24 November 1959 a meeting took place of an Air Ministry committee charged with considering further permanent Battle of Britain memorials as the 20th anniversary of the battle approached. The minutes, a draft of which exists in the BBFA files, considered various suggestions including the preservation of Biggin Hill, where, in addition to the memorial chapel, 'a museum could be established'. This idea was not proceeded with, although the proposal for a museum has emerged again in the twenty-first century, outside the auspices of the Ministry of Defence. Another possibility considered by the committee in 1959 was the naming of the new London Bridge as 'the Battle of Britain Bridge'.

A public house frequented by pilots, not least from Biggin Hill, was the White Hart in the village of Brasted. Many of them signed a blackout board of which a facsimile is kept at the much re-furbished pub. The original is at the Shoreham Aircraft Museum.

A major reunion of The Few took place at the White Hart in September 1969 at the time of the premiere of the *Battle of Britain* film. Those in the pub that day included: Ludwik Martel, Don Kingaby, 'Tich' Havercroft, 'Sailor' Malan, Douglas Bader, Bob Stanford Tuck, Bobby Deacon Elliott, Brian Kingcome, Norman Ryder, 'Bertie' Wootten, 'Gandy' Drobinski, Paddy Barthropp, Tony Bartley, Mike Duke-Woolley, Jack Rose and Johnny Kent.

The Battle of Britain Memorial Flight

The first name for what is now world famous as the Battle of Britain Memorial Flight was the Historic Aircraft Flight.

Wing Commander Peter Thompson, a veteran of the Battle of Britain, was the man who had the idea – in 1956 when he was Officer Commanding Biggin Hill – and he made sure that it happened.

According to his widow, Mimi, quoted in *Battle of Britain Memorial Flight – 50 years of flying*, by Jarrod Cotter:

> 'We held a showcase for the commemoration of the Battle of Britain every year and we would put on a huge display. It was very well attended, an enormous amount of people would turn up. It was a pageantry day as well as a memorial day. And I think really that was the beginning when my husband realised how many people were deeply interested in that period of our history.'

Thompson took steps, starting with the fact that he already had in his charge at Biggin Hill, and in flying condition, Hurricane llc, LF363.

Three Spitfires were acquired which had just ended their operational careers with the Temperature and Humidity Monitoring Flight (THUM), based at Hooton Park, Cheshire and Woodvale, Lancashire. There was a false start, when one of the aircraft crashed on take off from Woodvale. However, on 11 July 1957, PS853, PM631 and PS915 were flown from Duxford to Biggin Hill by Peter Thompson and two other World War Two fighter pilots, Group Captain 'Johnnie' Johnson, who had qualified for the Battle of Britain Clasp, and Group Captain Jamie Rankin.

Two Battle of Britain squadrons participated in the event when Hawker Hunters of No 41 Squadron and Gloster Javelins of No 46 Squadron joined the formation.

In an indication of immediate top level enthusiasm for the project, the Spitfires were greeted at Biggin Hill by Air Marshal Sir Thomas Pike, Air Officer, Commanding in Chief, Fighter Command.

However, these Spitfires had been built for photo reconnaissance duties and there was a strong feeling that there should be Spitfires designed for combat on the strength of the Flight. This was achieved when three aircraft were acquired, which, at that point, were far from airworthy, and had been used at the Royal Tournament in 1957 when a depiction of the wartime defence of Malta was one of the attractions.

On 15 September 1957 the Historic Aircraft Flight carried out a commemorative flight over Westminster Abbey, marking Battle of Britain Day.

The name of the unit was officially changed in February 1958 to Battle of Britain Flight and shortly afterwards a move took place to North Weald, followed by a period at Martlesham Heath. At this time considerable nervousness had developed over the advisability of relatively elderly aircraft flying over London. This was fuelled by a number of incidents.

It was announced that the Battle of Britain flypast over London on 20 September 1959 would be the last. During the event, Spitfire SL574, flown by a Battle of Britain Clasp holder, Air Vice-Marshal Harold Maguire, suffered engine failure. Maguire managed to put the aircraft down on the Oxo company sports ground at Bromley, Kent. A cricket match was in progress but the players had just gone off for tea. The incident naturally made headlines and seemed to reinforce the decision that had been taken to end the flypasts.

The next move for the Flight was to RAF Horsham St Faith, which today is Norwich Airport, then came transfer to Coltishall, also in Norfolk, in 1963.

There were frequent changes in the roster of aircraft, some of which were used during the making of the film, *Battle of Britain*. A noteworthy acquisition was Spitfire lla, P7350, which had taken part in the Battle of Britain with Nos 266 and 603 (City of Edinburgh) Squadrons.

The name, Battle of Britain Memorial Flight, was adopted officially on 1 June 1969. In 1973 Avro Lancaster PA474 was added to the strength of the BBMF, having been refurbished by its previous owner, RAF Waddington. The aircraft was named City of Lincoln, a choice which marked the association with the area of both the individual aircraft and the type.

In 1976 the Flight moved yet again, this time to Coningsby in Lincolnshire, which has remained its base ever since. A full time CO was appointed for the first time in 1977. Up until then the job of CO was a secondary duty for people in other mainline full-time jobs and the maintenance and flying was on a voluntary goodwill basis. Flypasts from time to time over London have taken place again since the 1980s.

For the 2014 season the fleet of aircraft consisted of six Spitfires, two Hurricanes, one Lancaster, two Chipmunks and one Dakota. Many flypasts and displays were arranged during the season.

The BBMF visitor centre at Coningsby is a partnership between the RAF and Lincolnshire County Council. Tours lasting about one hour are led by volunteer guides and there are education sessions for school children. Given the various rounds of 'defence cuts' over the years, the continued existence of this much loved part of the RAF always seems somewhat precarious.

Commonwealth War Graves Commission

The Imperial War Graves Commission was established in 1917 and, all over the world, cared for the graves of UK and Commonwealth military personnel lost in the two world wars. The key figure in its foundation was Fabian (later Sir Fabian) Ware (1869–1949), at one time editor of the *Morning Post* newspaper. Its funding comes mainly from the governments of the United Kingdom, Canada, Australia, New Zealand, South Africa and India. In 1960 the word 'Imperial' in its title was replaced with 'Commonwealth'.

The remains of many of the airmen who died in the Battle of Britain were, of course, discovered in and around the UK. At that time the policy of the IWGC was that men and women who died overseas should be buried in the country in which they had died or their remains had been found.

In the case of personnel to be buried in the UK families generally had the choice of where that burial would take place and whether the grave would be marked by a standard IWGC stone or by a stone provided by the family. Only graves marked by an IWGC stone would be maintained by the Commission.

Families were offered the chance to choose a short inscription to be placed on the stone. Sometimes familiar words were chosen – for example St John chapter 15, verse 13, which, in the King James version of the Bible, is rendered as, *'Greater Love have no man than this, that a man lay down his life for his friends'*. Also to be found are some of the most quoted words (or variations on them) from the 1914 poem by Laurence Binyon, 'For the Fallen' – *'At the going down of the sun and in the morning we will remember them.'*

Words specially composed in tribute to individuals include: *'In loving memory of Harry of Winnipeg, Manitoba, Canada. Nobly he lived, gloriously he died. We will remember him.'*

Grave of Pilot Officer Harry Davies Edwards, No 92 Squadron, at Hawkinge Cemetery, Kent. The Spitfire flown by Harry Edwards was shot down on 11 September 1940 and crashed at Evegate Manor Farm, Smeeth, near Ashford, Kent. However, his body was not found until 7 October. He was 24 years old.

'In love and gratitude to our dear son who was killed in the Battle of Britain. Mother.'

Grave of Sergeant Redvers Percival Hawkings, No 601 Squadron, at Filton (St Peter) churchyard, Gloucestershire. During combat over the Sussex coast on 18 August 1940 the Hurricane of Redvers Hawkings, aged 22, was shot down. It fell near Summer Lane, Nyetimber, Pagham.

Heartfelt tributes to Battle of Britain airmen also appear in cases where the man who was lost lies in a family grave.

On a family gravestone at Fulford Cemetery near York appears the inscription: *'To the glorious memory of our dearly loved son, Sergeant Pilot Malcolm Gray 72 (Fighter) Squadron (Spitfire) RAF, killed in action in Defence of Britain, September 5 1940, aged 20 years. Faithful unto Death.'*

Malcolm Gray was known as 'Mabel' on his squadron. His was one of three Spitfires from seventy-two shot down in combat with Messerschmitt Bf 109s on 5 September in the vicinity of Elham, near Folkestone. Pilot Officer 'Snowy' Winter was killed after baling out too low, but Flying Officer Des Sheen from Australia was wounded and survived.

Sergeant Gray's aircraft crashed into Elham Park Wood where two brothers, who had been working nearby, tried, without success, to drag him from the burning remains of the Spitfire.

In some cases a CWGC stone can be found on a grave which also has a family stone. Examples include Flight Sergeant N.T. Phillips (No 65 Squadron, killed in action 8 August 1940, Chatham Cemetery, Kent) and Sergeant Eric S. Bann (No 238 Squadron, killed in action 28 September 1940, Macclesfield Cemetery, Cheshire).

A unique case, amongst those who earned the Battle of Britain Clasp, is that of the grave at Windsor Road Cemetery, Bray, Berkshire of Pilot Officer Gerard Hamilton Maffett of No 257 Squadron. Gerry Maffett, a pre-war member of the RAFVR, was shot down by Messerschmitt Bf 109s over Clacton on 31 August 1940, his Hurricane crashing on the foreshore near Walton-on-the-Naze.

As was often the case, his grave was initially marked by the IWGC with a temporary wooden cross. Gerry Maffett's mother, who would live to be 100 and died in 1975, requested that this cross remain in place on the family grave, rather than being taken away when a headstone was provided.

Around the time of the Millennium the Maffett family realised that the inevitable deterioration in the condition of the cross was becoming serious. Discussions took place with the CWGC and Bray Parish Council. The outcome was explained at the time by Sean Maffett, Gerry's nephew and a former RAF officer himself. He commented:

> 'Refurbishment was not the right option because that would detract from historic authenticity. We decided on a transparent plastic shelter, but one that was near invisible as possible. It would keep rain off the cross, but also allow air to circulate. The War Graves Commisison did an excellent job of designing and building it and we hope that the wood and paintwork of the cross, which has turned out to be remarkably tough, will survive in its near orginal state.'

Personnel who served in the RAF in the Second World War, with no known grave, are remembered on various memorials around the world, depending on the geographical area from which they went missing. Those of The Few, lost in the Battle of Britain, whose place of burial is not known are commemorated on the Runnymede Memorial, at Cooper's Hill, overlooking the Thames at Englefield Green between Windsor and Egham. This memorial, the responsibility of the CWGC, contains the names of over 20,000 personnel who were lost flying from airfields in the United Kingdom and northern and western Europe.

The memorial was designed by Edward (later Sir Edward) Maufe with sculpture by Vernon Hill. It was opened by Her Majesty the Queen on 17 October 1953 and can be visited every day apart from Christmas Day and New Year's Day.

Edward Maufe had been born in 1882 with the surname Muff, but changed the name by deed poll in his twenties. He was an officer in the Royal Artillery in the First World War. As an architect with his own practice, Maufe came under the influence of the Arts and Crafts Movement. His work included the Palace of Industry at the Wembley exhibition of 1924, Kelling Hall in Norfolk, Guildford Cathedral and the rebuilding of the Middle Temple and Gray's Inn in London, after both had suffered Second World War bomb damage.

Between 1943 and 1969 Maufe was first Principal Architect UK and then Chief Architect and Artistic Adviser to the Imperial War Graves Commission which administers the Runnymede Memorial. His services to the IWGC brought Maufe a knighthood in 1954. He died in 1974.

From the speech made by the Queen at the opening of the Runnymede Memorial:

'*This memorial has been built in proud memory of the men and women of the Air Forces of the British Commonwealth and Empire who lost their lives serving from bases in the United Kingdom and North West Europe and have no known graves.*

'*They were part of a glorious and far larger company who laid down their lives for freedom: and this memorial is one of many others built, wherever the battle raged, so that they may not be forgotten. Twenty thousand, four hundred and fifty-five names are recorded on these stones: and all races and countries of the British Commonwealth have here their representatives.*

'*It is very fitting that those who rest in nameless graves should be remembered in this place. For it was in these fields of Runnymede seven centuries ago that our forefathers first planted a seed of liberty which helped to spread across the earth the conviction that man should be free and not enslaved. And when the life of this belief was threatened by the iron hand of tyranny, their successors came forward without hesitation to fight, and if it was demanded of them, to die for its salvation. As only free men can, they knew the value of that for which they fought, and that the price was worth paying.*

'They were not alone in this knowledge, and in this sacrifice. At this very hour a memorial porch is being unveiled in Chelmsford Cathedral to commemorate some of those American airmen who fought together with us against the same aggression.

'With prophetic insight, Pope wrote of this hill on which we stand:

> *"On Cooper's Hill eternal wreaths shall grow*
> *While lasts the mountain, or while Thames shall flow"*

'Indeed the heroism of each will be remembered as long as this memorial shall stand. But that which was done by all will, with God's help, still be remembered when these stones have crumbled into dust. For wherever and for as long as freedom flourishes on the earth, the men and women who possess it will thank them and will say that they did not die in vain. This is their true and everlasting memorial.'

The largest CWGC cemetery in Britain is the Brookwood Military Cemetery near Woking in Surrey. In 37 acres are the graves of over 5,000 service men and women including a signficant number of men who flew in the Battle of Britain.

The privately-owned Brookwood Cemetery as a whole is the largest in Britain and claims to be one of the largest in the world. Its owners describe it as, 'a working cemetery for all denominations and nationalities from all over the world'.

The cemetery is classified by English Heritage as a Grade 1 historic park and garden. There is an active and voluntarily-run Brookwood Cemetery Society which promotes interest in the cemetery, organises events and produces publications.

For many years funeral trains were run to Brookwood from a special station at Waterloo in London. These trains were operated by the London and South Western Railway and, from 1923, the Southern Railway. They ceased after the London terminus was bombed in April 1941.

In the words of the cemetery society:

'Brookwood is vast — almost rural — and is quite unlike any of the other London cemeteries it was designed to surpass and replace. The bold imaginative planting (which includes several avenues of giant sequoia) has now matured. The Cemetery deserves to be recognised as a site of national historical importance and has the potential to become a World Heritage Site.'

Battle of Britain Day – 15 September

Commemorations of the Battle of Britain in September each year began very quickly after the battle. Early formalization of the principle appears in Home Security Circular No 138/1943, dated 24 August 1943 and headed, 'Battle of Britain Sunday'. This announced that:

'His Majesty the King has approved a proposal that Civil Defence Day, which would have been held this year, shall be combined with the Royal Air Force Commemorations of the Battle of Britain, and Sunday 26th September, 1943 has been appointed to be observed as Battle of Britain Sunday.'

Services of remembrance and thanksgiving were being held around the country, as they had been the year before.

The service was held at St Paul's Cathedral and detailed arrangements for a parade in London on this 'Day of National Thanksgiving' were later issued by Air Vice-Marshal D. Harries, Director General of Personal Services. A wide range of military and civilian personnel were to take part.

Enemy action was still a possibility. The arrangements for the parade were regarded as secret. A paragraph in the Harries document instructed that:

'In the event of an alert being sounded on the sirens the march will continue. Should an actual attack develop, whether the sirens have sounded or not, the column will split into right and left columns and march on either side of the street, close up to the buildings where they exist.'

From 1944 services were held in Westminster Abbey.

Despite competing claims of other days 15 September came to be thought of as a particularly momentous point in the fighting. The day has been marked on an annual basis, with commemorations of varying intensity, over the years.

The Sunday on or after 15 September is the date on which is held the service of commemoration in Westminster Abbey.

The date was summarised by Wood and Dempster in *The Narrow Margin* as: '*Heavy attacks on London, broken up by Fighter Command. Highest German losses since August 18. Serious rethinking by German High Command.*' They went on to postulate that Sunday 15 September '*was remarkable for its ultimate change of German policy and not for its heavy losses, as the 185 German aircraft claimed (by the RAF) would lead many to believe.*'

The weather was mostly fine and the Germans regarded that Sunday at the end of the summer of 1940, as providing another opportunity for striking a major blow against Fighter Command and British morale, in the run up to invasion.

Early in the day there were Luftwaffe reconnaissance sorties, a standard feature of German activity in the first part of the morning. The attacks started at about 11am, with major enemy formations building up over Calais and Boulogne. '*The stupidity of large formations sorting themselves out in full view of British radar was not yet realised by the Luftwaffe,*' commented Wood and Dempster.

Fighter Command Hurricane and Spitfire squadrons engaged the formations, at heights varying by 11,000ft, over Kent.

Generally the German force was broken up and bombs fell over a wide area of central London and the southern suburbs. In the early afternoon another major attack developed.

Other targets during the day included the Supermarine works at Woolston, Southampton and the naval base at Portland, Dorset.

Though the British claims for victories on 15 September were a gross exaggeration, nonetheless by the end of the day the wreckage of German aircraft lay scattered across the south-east.

In the years after the Second World War the remembrance of the battle was regarded as lasting for a week with 15 September as the key date. Programmes of events were organised, often by RAFA centrally or by individual branches, as well as by RAF stations.

The brochure produced by RAFA in 1953 declared that:

'Britain has set aside each year, in the month of September, a week to be commemorated as Battle of Britain Week, with 15th September as the day marking the crux of the whole conflict. It will be ever honoured and recalled

as the people of these islands gather in their cathedrals and churches, on Royal Air Force airfields, in public places and, as yet, often in quiet thought within their own homes, to pay tribute and to renew their thanks to the Few, who by daring skill and self-sacrifice, brought deliverance to the many.'

Later in the same article there was reference to *'a third nation-wide Wings Day appeal to ensure that there are funds from which to aid the sick and needy, including the widows and dependants of personnel of the British and Commonwealth Air Forces.'*

The same brochure listed seventy-one RAF stations that were 'among the many' that would be 'At Home' to the general public on Sunday, 19 September 1953. Across the Home Commands, they included Biggin Hill, Tangmere, Odiham, West Malling, Coningsby, Binbrook, Marham, Scampton, Kinloss, Benson, Hendon, Little Rissington, Thorney Island, Weston Zoyland, Debden and Aston Down. Today RAFA continues to run The Wings Appeal as its 'on going fund raising campaign that runs throughout the year'.

Flypasts

On 15 September 1945 the fifth anniversary of the Battle of Britain was commemorated by a flypast over London, in which a considerable number of veterans of the battle participated. They were led by Douglas Bader and others to fly included: Billy Drake, Keith Lofts, Roy Bush, Pete Brothers, John Ellis, Frank Carey, Tim Vigors, Denis Crowley-Milling and 'Hawkeye' Wells. The flypast also featured No 247 Squadron, which had taken part in the battle, but in 1945 was flying de Havilland Vampires.

The flypast became an annual event. Tragedy struck on 11 September 1953, when a rehearsal was being led by a Gloster Meteor flown by New Zealand battle veteran, Wing Commander Bobby Yule, OC RAF Horsham St Faith. Above south-east London another Meteor in the formation struck Yule's aircraft. His Meteor fell away from the formation and it appears that, over a densely populated area, he made no attempt to escape. Instead Yule tried to bring the crippled aircraft down amongst the buildings at the Royal Arsenal, Woolwich.

Bobby Yule died in the subsequent crash, despite attempts by Arsenal personnel to rescue him from the burning wreckage. In September 1993 a memorial to him was unveiled in the officers' mess at the Royal Arsenal by his two sons who had followed him into the RAF.

In the following years there were considerable concerns about the perceived dangers of flying Second World War aircraft over London. It was announced that the 1959 Battle of Britain flypast would be the last. During that event a Spitfire forced-landed on the Oxo company sports ground at Bromley, Kent. (See also Battle of Britain Memorial Flight in this section.)

In more recent years, of course, the historic aircraft of the Battle of Britain Memorial Flight have been a regular sight over London, with no mishaps.

Royal Air Force Museum, Hendon

The main site of the RAF Museum is situated on what was once Hendon airfield. Here the Battle of Britain Hall, refurbished for the 70th anniversary of the battle, 'tells the story of the world's first decisive air battle'. A sound and light show explains what happened and a number of aircraft are displayed. There is a permanent exhibition, Art and the Battle of Britain.

Fleet Air Arm Memorial, Lee-on-Solent

The memorial, on Marine Parade West in the Hampshire town, commemorates 1,925 Fleet Air Arm personnel who were lost in the Second World War and have no known grave. Some of those remembered earned the Battle of Britain Clasp, either with the two FAA squadrons that took part or on attachment to RAF Fighter Command units.

Constructed by the Imperial War Graves Commission, the memorial was unveiled on 20 May 1953 by the then Duchess of Kent.

Rolls-Royce Memorial Window, Derby

The window, at the Rolls-Royce factory, Derby, was unveiled by Marshal of the Royal Air Force Lord Tedder, Chief of the Air Staff, in January 1949 in the presence of a large number of The Few. Rolls-Royce and its staff had played a key part in winning the Battle of Britain, particularly through the provision of Merlin engines for Hurricanes and Spitfires. The artist for the window was Hugh Easton, much associated with commemoration of the battle, including his work on the Westminster Abbey window.

In mid-2014 the Rolls-Royce window had been in storage for some years, but plans were being made for it to be put up again in 2015, although the precise location had not been decided.

The Guinea Pig Club

During the Second World War many aircrew disfigured by burns and other injuries were treated at the Queen Victoria Hospital, East Grinstead by the team led by plastic surgeon, Archie McIndoe, a New Zealander. Many of his early patients needed plastic surgery as a result of injuries suffered in the Battle of Britain.

In June 1941 a number of The Few were prominent in the founding of The Guinea Pig Club at the hospital. Tom Gleave, later a leading member of the BBFA, was one of them and as he explained in 1992:

> 'Archie generated a bond of fellowship in which rank was forgotten. He believed that nothing should stand in the way of making terribly mutilated human beings whole again and so we had much more freedom than was traditional in military or medical circles.
>
> 'Local people had to get used to the sight of us walking out to the pubs in the evenings, those who were lame or in wheelchairs assisted by those whose worst problem might be a considerably re-arranged face. Archie wanted to boost our confidence and help us achieve our common ambition to get back into the war. He invited us into the operating theatre to watch him at work and it was there that we began to mutter "guinea pig."'

According to the present Blond McIndoe Research Foundation:

> 'The camaraderie and quite often the black humour was integral to the club and often needed to help the members through difficult times. Not only did they have to overcome the physical hardship but also psychological. For some members their disfigured features were too much for their wives and girlfriends to cope with and their pre war relationships ended at a most traumatic time. However a number of them ended up marrying nurses from the hospital as they got used to seeing past their injuries.'

Archie McIndoe was knighted in 1947 and died in 1960. In 2014 a statue of him was unveiled in East Grinstead by HRH The Princess Royal.

Over the years many of The Few who died during the course of the battle have been commemorated with memorials at or close to the locations where their aircraft crashed. Others have been remembered who survived the battle but were killed later. Some examples of those so remembered are:

Sergeant Robert Fraser

Bobby Fraser was a pre-war member of the RAFVR who joined No 257 Squadron when it was re-formed at Hendon in May 1940. He was credited with probably destroying a Messerschmitt Bf 110 on 3 September 1940. On 22 October he was shot down over Folkestone in combat with Messerschmitt Bf 109s, his Hurricane crashing into a wood at Moat Farm, Shadoxhurst, near Ashford. Fraser was 20. He was buried in Craigton Cemetery, Glasgow.

In 2013 the owner of Moat Farm was Michael Bax, at the time the High Sherriff of Kent, and it was his idea that a memorial should be erected in the wood adjacent to the site of the crash. A service and unveiling took place on 4 April 2013.

Flight Lieutenant Charles Grayson

Charles Grayson was educated at Uckfield Grammar School in Sussex. He joined the RAF in 1929 as an aircraft apprentice and became a metal rigger. He was later accepted for pilot training and, having qualified, served with No 23 Squadron.

Grayson joined No 213 Squadron on 8 March 1937. He was part of a detachment of 213 which went to Merville in France on 17 May 1940. He was attached to No 229 Squadron in France on 20 May but rejoined 213 Squadron in England a few days later.

Over Dunkirk on 29 May he was credited with destroying a Ju 87 and probably an He 111. On 12 August he claimed a Bf 110 destroyed off the Isle of Wight. By this time a flight sergeant, he made his last flight with 213 Squadron on 30 October 1940.

Charles Grayson was commissioned from Warrant Officer in June 1941 and served in Coastal Command. On 8 July 1945, serving with No 53 Squadron, Flight Lieutenant Grayson was the pilot of a Liberator involved in night circuit training from St Davids, Pembrokeshire. The aircraft suffered engine failure and crashed on White Sands Road, near Emlych Farm, killing the crew. A slate memorial was unveiled at the crash site in 1995, provided by the Pembrokeshire Aviation Group.

Charles Grayson was 32 and is buried in Lewes Cemetery, Sussex. His name appears on the Roll of Honour of Halton apprentices who died in the Second World War, kept at St George's Church, Halton, Buckinghamshire.

Flying Officer Oswald Pigg

A memorial unveiled in a restaurant in Kent in 2012 paid tribute to Flying Officer Oswald St John 'Ossie' Pigg of No 72 Squadron. Pigg was shot down in combat with Messerschmitt Bf 109s on 1 September 1940, his Spitfire crashing and burning out at Elvey Farm, Pluckley, near Ashford. The remains of the pilot were recovered and he was laid to rest in St Oswald's burial ground, Durham.

The memorial plaque was placed close to the crash site in what is now the Elvey Farm Hotel. The unveiling was carried out by Ossie Pigg's niece Stephanie Haigh, accompanied by other members of the family. Tribute was paid by Wing Commander Bob Foster, Chairman of the Battle of Britain Fighter Assocation. Representatives of 72 Squadron at the ceremony, organised by the Battle of Britain Memorial Trust, included Air Chief Marshal Sir John Day, a former CO of the squadron.

Oswald Pigg, born in 1918, was the son of a clergyman and was educated at the Royal Grammar School, Newcastle-upon-Tyne. After joining the RAF on a short service commission, he had begun his training in May 1937. Later that year he joined No 72 Squadron which was then based at Church Fenton and flying Gloster Gladiators. The squadron began to receive Spitfires in April 1939.

On 2 June 1940, during the fighting over Dunkirk, Pigg shot down a Junkers Ju 87 'Stuka', but his aircraft was hit by fire from another Stuka and he was wounded in the leg. He made a belly landing on the aerodrome at Gravesend where No 72 Squadron had arrived the day before. On 5 June the squadron was moved temporarily out of the front line, with a transfer to Acklington, Northumberland.

It was on 15 August that the Luftwaffe attacked north-east England, suffering casualties which would contribute to the German airmen regarding that day as 'Black Thursday'. A return to the south came on 31 August when 72 Squadron was ordered to Biggin Hill, but with that sector station having suffered grievous damage, Croydon became a temporary home from the first day of September.

Pilot Officer A.E.A.D.J.G. van den Hove d'Ertsenrijck

Members of Albert Emmanuel Alix Dieudonne Jean Ghislain van den Hove d'Ertsenrijck's family have produced an account of his life, as one of the overseas airmen who came to Britain's aid in 1940.

'*He was born in Charleroi, Belgium in 1908. He attended St Louis School in Liège and then St Michel School in Brussels. On December 3 1928 he joined the Belgian Air Force, carrying out basic infantry and cavalry training as part of the 74th entry then moving to the air force itself on December 26 1930. He served as an observer, before qualifying as a pilot in 1932. His first operational posting was to a unit equipped with Fairey Fireflys.*

'*After time as an instructor he returned to his former squadron which by now had received Hawker Hurricanes. The squadron was coming to readiness on May 10 1940 when successive dawn attacks by Me 110s destroyed all but two of the Hurricanes, only van den Hove and one other being able to take off. Van den Hove intercepted a raid by twin-engine bombers on Brussels and damaged one. He went on to land at Beauvechain where his aircraft was destroyed on the ground the following day.*

'*There followed a chaotic withdrawal by road and train to the south of France, where it was intended that they should re-equip at Mauguio near Montpelier and continue the fight. On the June 19 the senior Belgian officer announced that they were expected to surrender, van den Hove and several others decided to ignore this and make their way to England. They took two vehicles and some mess funds and set off for Port Vendres near the Spanish border. Ludicrously they were branded as thieves and deserters by the Belgians, these charges only being dropped in 1948.*

'*With the assistance of Royal Navy officers and the Belgian embassy in England they were able to board the SS* Apapa *and leave as part of a convoy on June 24, arriving at Liverpool via Gibraltar on July 7. Their next stop was the Belgian reception centre at Tenby, south-west Wales. Van den Hove, who could speak little English, was commissioned in the RAF on July 19 and sent to No 7 OTU Hawarden on the 21st.*

'*He was posted to No 43 Squadron at Tangmere on August 5. He claimed a Junkers Ju 87 destroyed on the 16th, a Bf 109 on the 26th and a Bf 110 on September 4. In this latter combat his glycol tank was damaged and he made a forced-landing at Ford, following a mid-air fire.*

Pilot Officers Bill Millington (left) and Tom Neil of No 249 Squadron during the Battle of Britain. Neil survived the war, but Millington, an Australian born in England, was killed in action on 30 October 1940 and is remembered on Panel 9 of the Runnymede Memorial.

Hurricane LF363 and Spitfire P7350 of the Battle of Britain Memorial Flight perform over Capel-le-Ferne in 2012. At the time they were in the guise of other aircraft, which had flown in the Battle of Britain. *(Barry Duffield)*

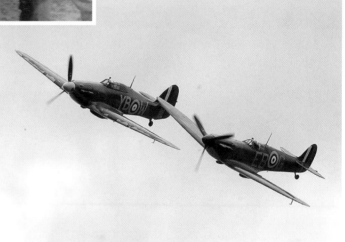

Squadron Leader Michael Wainwright studies the names on the Christopher Foxley-Norris Wall at the National Memorial to The Few, Capel-le-Ferne. In the Battle of Britain Flying Officer Wainwright was a Spitfire pilot with No 64 Squadron. *(Barry Duffield)*

HRH Prince Michael of Kent at the National Memorial to The Few, Capel-le-Ferne. *(Barry Duffield)*

HRH the Prince of Wales at the opening of the Battle of Britain London Monument in 2005. *(Courtesy Edward McManus)*

At Crackington Haven in Cornwall, land was donated to the National Trust in memory of Denis Parnall and all who fought and died in the Battle of Britain. *(Jeff Cherrington, National Trust)*

A coveted award. The 1939–1945 Star with Battle of Britain Clasp. *(BBFA)*

From left to right, Wing Commander Bob Foster, Air Commodore 'Pete' Brothers and Squadron Leader 'Bam' Bamberger. They are all wearing the 1939–1945 Star with Battle of Britain Clasp and the tie of the Battle of Britain Fighter Association. *(Battle of Britain Memorial Trust)*

Scenes from early post-war Battle of Britain reunions. Lord Dowding is in the centre of the second picture. *(Courtesy Flying Officer Ken Wilkinson)*

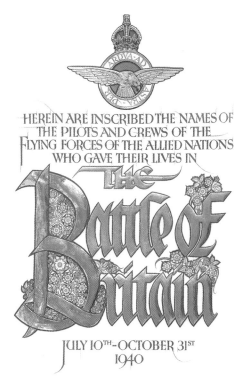

HEREIN ARE INSCRIBED THE NAMES OF
THE PILOTS AND CREWS OF THE
FLYING FORCES OF THE ALLIED NATIONS
WHO GAVE THEIR LIVES IN

The Battle of Britain

JULY 10TH – OCTOBER 31ST
1940

The RAF Chapel and Battle of Britain window at Westminster Abbey. *(Dean and Chapter of Westminster)*

The Battle of Britain Roll of Honour held at Westminster Abbey. *(Dean and Chapter of Westminster)*

Close to RAF Northolt is the Polish Memorial. Men who flew in the Battle of Britain are commemorated here. *(Wing Commander Andy Simpson)*

A road in the Jersey parish of St Ouen was named Rue Henri Gonay in 2014. Squadron Leader Gonay, a Belgian, had flown in the Battle of Britain with No 235 Squadron. He was killed in action in 1944, his aircraft crashing near this spot. *(Bernie Morel)*

CWGC graves, including those of Battle of Britain airmen, at North Weald Bassett (St Andrew) churchyard in Essex. *(Wing Commander Andy Simpson)*

Pilot Officer Kenneth Manger fought over Dunkirk and in the Battle of Britain with No 17 Squadron. He was awarded the DFC and became a member of the Caterpillar Club after parachuting into the Channel. On 11 August 1940 his Hurricane did not return from combat with Messerschmitt Bf 109s. His name appears on Panel 9 of the Runnymede Memorial. In 1999 a plaque in his memory was unveiled at The Crossley Heath School in his native Halifax, West Yorkshire. *(Courtesy Manger family via Edward McManus)*

The two logbook entries for 25 October 1940 that indicate that 'Alastair' Ogilvy was one of The Few. The term X raid meant unidentified aircraft detected by Chain Home or the Observer Corps. *(Courtesy of Edward McManus)*

'Alastair' Ogilvy's medals, ribbons and miniatures including the 1939-1945 Star with Battle of Britain Clasp. *(Courtesy of Edward McManus)*

The altar at St George's Chapel, Biggin Hill. *(Wing Commander Andy Simpson)*

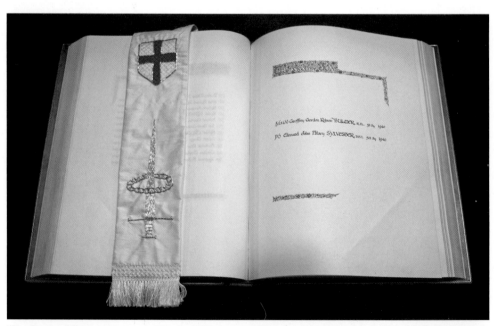

The Book of Remembrance at Biggin Hill, open at the page recording the death of Sub-Lieutenant Geoffrey Bulmer, RN. *(Wing Commander Andy Simpson)*

In the restored filter room at Bentley Priory. *(Bentley Priory Battle of Britain Trust)*

The unveiling, in 2013 of a memorial to Sergeant Bobby Fraser, close to the spot at Shadoxhurst, Kent where his Hurricane crashed. On the left is Michael Bax, High Sheriff of Kent at the time and on the right Wing Commander Bob Foster, Chairman of the Battle of Britain Fighter Association. *(Barry Duffield)*

Royal Navy pilots who lost their lives in the Battle of Britain and have no known grave are among those remembered on the Fleet Air Arm Memorial at Lee-on-Solent, Hampshire. *(Wing Commander Andy Simpson)*

The grave of Pilot Officer Gerard Maffett at Bray, Berkshire is the only one from the Battle of Britain still marked by an IWGC wooden cross, at the request of his mother. Gerry Maffett was killed in action on 31 August 1940, serving with No 257 Squadron. Long after the war the wreckage of his Hurricane was recovered from the foreshore at Walton-on-the-Naze, Essex and is now in the collection of the RAF Museum, Hendon. *(Wing Commander Andy Simpson)*

Part of the stained glass window at St Margaret's Church, Wrenbury, Cheshire, commemorating those of the parish who died in the Second World War. Sergeant Fred Eley was killed in action with No 74 Squadron in the Battle of Britain. *(David Moores)*

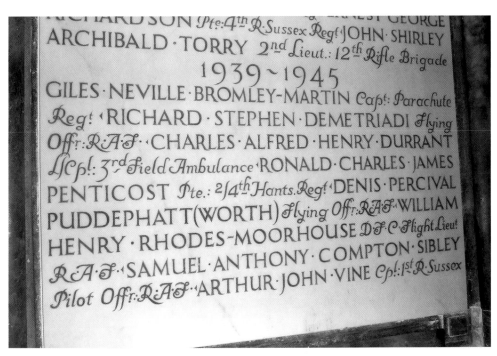

Two men who fought and died in the Battle of Britain are commemorated at St Martin's church, Westmeston, Sussex. Richard Stephen Demetriadi and William Henry Rhodes-Moorhouse were brothers-in-law and served with No 601 Squadron. *(Edward McManus)*

The lonely memorial on Romney Marsh to Pilot Officer Arthur Clarke of No 504 Squadron. Though smaller, it is in the style of a CWGC headstone. *(Group Captain Patrick Tootal)*

The grave of Pilot Officer 'Pip' Cardell, at Great Paxton, Huntingdonshire, marked by a sundial. *(Wing Commander Andy Simpson)*

Pilot Officer 'Pip' Cardell.

Many men who flew in the Battle of Britain are remembered on memorials around the world. Flying Officer J.J.F.H. Bandinel qualified for the Battle of Britain Clasp with No 3 Squadron. He was lost in December 1941, over the Western Desert, while serving with No 260 Squadron and, with no known grave, his name appears on the Alamein memorial. (Edward McManus)

August 1940. The funeral of Pilot Officer W.M.L. Fiske at Boxgrove (SS Mary and Blaise) churchyard, Sussex, also known as Boxgrove Priory. Fiske, an American citizen, was wounded in action on 16 August and died the next day. He has a memorial window in the Priory and a memorial in St Paul's Cathedral.

Each year a commemoration is held at the memorial at Chart Sutton, Kent, where a No 1 Squadron Hurricane crashed on 3 September 1940. The pilot, who did not survive, was Pilot Officer Robert Shaw. *(Wing Commander Andy Simpson)*

One of the plaques remembering Battle of Britain airmen now displayed in schools. It was unveiled at Lancing College, West Sussex in 2014. *(Battle of Britain Historical Society)*

Grave stones often refer to an airman's status as one of The Few. Air Commodore 'Jimmy' Fenton commanded No 238 Squadron in the battle and is buried in the churchyard at St Brelade, Jersey.

Battle of Britain class steam locomotive, No 34084 *253 Squadron* at Ashford on 20 April 1957, heading the *Man of Kent* express from Charing Cross to Margate. *(Dr Ben Brooksbank)*

The Kenley airfield memorial in a former blast pen. *(Richard Hunting)*

Former Warrant Officer 'Dave' Denchfield at Hemel Hempstead School in 2011 with the plaque unveiled in his honour. Sergeant Denchfield qualified for the Battle of Britain Clasp flying Spitfires with No 610 Squadron. He died in 2012.

'Dave' Denchfield was one of the many veterans of 1940 shot down over the Continent in the following year. He was photographed at St Omer in February 1941 shortly after he had baled out.

'On the morning of September 7 van den Hove appeared in a well known photograph outside the officers' mess at Tangmere. The occasion was a visit to the Squadron by Squadron Leader George Lott, its former CO who had been badly wounded on July 9 1940. Two of the pilots pictured with him, Squadron Leader Caesar Hull (appointed CO on September 1) and Flight Lieutenant Dick Reynell were killed in action later in the day.

'On September 11 van den Hove was posted to 501 Squadron at Kenley. On the 15th, his first patrol with the squadron, he was shot down by Me109s during an attack on Do 17s. An eye witness saw his Hurricane, P 2760, attempt a forced landing in a meadow adjacent to the River Stour where it passes through Olantigh Park near Wye in Kent. The pilot was seen to be leaving the cockpit with his parachute unstrapped but fell dead in the river after falling through the branches.'

Pilot Officer van den Hove d'Ertsenrijck was 32. He was buried in St Stephen's churchyard, Lympne, Kent. On 20 October 1949 his remains were exhumed and re-interred in the Pelouse d'Honneur Cemetery of Brussels at Evere. The site of the grave at Lympne is still marked. In August 2010 members of the family unveiled a memorial to him close to his crash site.

The Polish Air Force Memorial, Northolt

The number of Polish airmen who flew in the Battle of Britain was about 145, more than any other overseas nationality. Two men who had served as Chiefs of the Air Staff, Viscounts Trenchard and Portal, were leaders in the campaign to raise money for a Polish memorial at the end of the war. 'They lived with us and died with us in all the battles of the war and Northolt was their main station,' wrote Trenchard.

The money was raised and the site chosen at Western Avenue, Northolt. The sculptor was Mieczyslaw Lubelski, who had survived the Warsaw uprising and concentration camp incarceration. The memorial he produced consists of three stone slabs, one of which is placed vertically, with an eagle about to take off at its top. Inscribed are the names of Polish airmen lost in action, including in the Battle of Britain, though not those who died in other ways, such as through accidents.

The Battle of Britain Pilot's Memorial Garden, Parkhouse Farm, Chart Sutton, Kent

At about 11.30am on 3 September 1940 a Hurricane crashed on the edge of an orchard at Parkhouse Farm, Chart Sutton, overlooking the Weald near Maidstone. Although no identification was made at the time, it can now be accepted that the aircraft that fell was Hurricane P 3782 of No 1 Squadron and the pilot who was killed was Pilot Officer Robert Shaw.

Mrs Underdown, who was picking hops at Manor Farm nearby, with members of her family, saw the crashing Hurricane, was concerned that her house might have been hit and sent her daughter Win to find out.

Win's niece Rita Clarke (nee Holland) wrote:

'On the way she met Elizabeth Wheatley from the big house next to Chart church and both girls ran down through the orchards. They met a scene of fire and devastation – scattered wreckage and exploding ammunition. They were there before the arrival of the police and Army. There was nothing to be done.'

With the permission of the farmer, an elderly couple living nearby placed a cross at the scene, planted flowers and maintained the garden they had created until they died. After a period of neglect, the garden was cared for by Win's brother, George Underdown and other members of the family assisted when he suffered poor health. Up to seventeen boxes of bedding plants were placed in the garden each year.

From 1970 the Headcorn branch of the Royal Air Forces Association has organised an annual commemoration in Chart Sutton.

In 2013, when the garden had just been re-furbished, this took the form of a service in the church, followed by a ceremony at the garden. Members of Robert Shaw's family were present.

Roadside Memorials

Romney Marsh

A small memorial, in the style of a CWGC headstone and often enhanced by flowers, stands at the side of a road on Romney Marsh, south of the village of Newchurch and not far from a house named 'Rookelands'. The memorial perpetuates the memory of Pilot Officer Arthur William Clarke, of No

504 Squadron, whose Hurricane was shot down over the Kent coast on 11 September 1940 and fell close to where the memorial now stands.

Arthur Clarke had been born in Altrincham, Cheshire on Boxing Day 1919. He had a highly successful career at Cheadle Hulme School, becoming captain of lacrosse, leader of the school scout group, a house captain and school captain. He was presented with the John Rylands gold watch. His name was later included on the school war memorial. A contemporary of Clarke's at the school had a similar name, though the 'Arthur' and 'William' were reversed. Those at the school at the time remembered that the headmaster had a standard joke of muddling up the two boys.

Having left the school in 1938 and worked for the Metrological Department of the Air Ministry, Arthur Clarke joined the RAF on a short service commission in June 1939. After converting to Hurricanes he joined No 504 Squadron on 13 April 1940, a day on which the squadron was transferred from Debden to Martlesham Heath. Various other moves, including to France, took place. On 11 September the squadron was flying from Hendon.

About 4pm on that day, Pilot Officer Clarke's aircraft crashed and burned out. No remains were found and his name was eventually placed on the Runnymede Memorial. No fellow pilots saw the aircraft go down. The CO, Squadron Leader John Sample, wrote to Arthur Clarke's mother describing the circumstances as best he could, but admitting: *'As nobody saw anything one can really not say what happened.'* Sample added: *'We all liked him very much and are very sorry he is not with us now.'*

Post war excavation of the site revealed personal items, including a handkerchief with the name 'Clarke' written on it. Human remains were found, as well as proof of the identity of the aircraft. The remains were left where they were and Arthur Clarke's family arranged for the memorial to be put in place.

It was dedicated on 11 September 1986. A wreath was laid by Flight Lieutenant Symon Riley, a Tornado navigator and great nephew of Arthur Clarke.

Woolverton, Somerset

A memorial on a grass verge, opposite the Red Lion Inn, Woolverton, reads:

In Memory of
Kenneth Christopher Holland
RIPLEY
Sergeant Pilot RAF
Killed in action 25 Sept 1940
This stone marks the spot where
he fell after having destroyed
an enemy Heinkel

Kenneth Christopher Holland was born and grew up in New South Wales. His relationship with his parents was strained and after he met an Englishman, 'Toby' Ripley, it was agreed that Mr Ripley should act as Ken Holland's guardian.

Toby Ripley bought a house at Camelford, Cornwall, where Ken Holland lived. He used the name 'Ripley' and hoped to be formally adopted, however this never happened. When Ken Holland joined the RAFVR in 1939 he did so under his birth name. After converting to Spitfires, Sergeant Holland joined No 152 Squadron at Warmwell on 1 August 1940.

The circumstances of his death are described in the book *Men of the Battle of Britain*:

'On the 25th (of September 1940) Holland attacked a He 111 and set it on fire. Seeing a parachute, he went in for a closer look but was shot down by a gunner still in the stricken Heinkel. His Spitfire, N 3173, crashed near Church Farm, Woolverton, Somerset. Holland was found to have been shot in the head. The Heinkel crashed at Church Farm. Four of the crew were killed, only the pilot baling out and being captured.

'Holland was cremated at Weymouth Crematorium. Mr Ripley had a memorial stone placed near the site of the crash. In 1976 the stone was moved. It is now on a grass verge opposite the Red Lion Inn, Woolverton, close to the village war memorial.

In late 2013 the lettering was becoming faded.

Shoreham Aircraft Museum memorial project

In 2006 the Shoreham Aircraft Museum launched a plan to provide memorials at Battle of Britain crash sites. By 2013 seven had been dedicated. Those remembered are:

Acting Flight Lieutenant Jimmy Paterson, a New Zealander, killed in action with No 92 Squadron, 27 September 1940. Memorial at Sparepenny Lane, Farningham, Kent.

Flying Officer 'Nat' Barry of South Africa, No 501 Squadron, 7 October 1940. Memorial at Court Lodge Farm, Darenth, Kent.

Sergeant Trevor Oldfield, No 92 Squadron, 27 September 1940. Memorial at Hesketh Park, Dartford, Kent.

Sergeant Hugh Ellis, No 85 Squadron, 1 September 1940. Memorial at Warren Road, Chelsfield, Kent.

Flight Lieutenant Pat Hughes DFC, Australian with No 234 Squadron, 7 September 1940. Memorial at Main Road, Sundridge, Kent.

Flying Officer Robin 'Bubble' Waterston, No 603 Squadron, 31 August 1940. Memorial at Repository Road, Woolwich Common, south-east London.

Flight Lieutenant 'Dickie' Reynell, Australian, No 43 Squadron. 7 September 1940. Memorial at Point Hill Park, Blackheath, south-east London.

'To the treasured memory of
Our beloved son
Sgt Pilot Trevor Guest Oldfield
Killed in action
Sept 27th 1940, aged 21 years
Not just to-day but every day in silence
We remember'

From Trevor Oldfield's gravestone at St Stephen's Church burial ground, Chertsey, Surrey.

St Clement Danes and the Lord Dowding statue

The RAF website points out that for over 1,000 years a church has stood on the spot in The Strand in London where St Clement Danes stands today. The name is traditionally said to derive from the fact that it was originally built by Danes expelled from the City of London by King Alfred in the ninth century.

The church is mentioned in the Domesday Book and for nearly 150 years was in the care of the Knights Templar. It was not damaged in the Great Fire of London in 1666 but was rebuilt in 1681 by Christopher Wren and a steeple was added to the tower by James Gibbs in the early eighteenth century.

On 10 May 1941, right at the end of the 1940/41 Blitz, incendiary bombs caused the building to be gutted leaving only the walls and tower standing. Twelve years later the Air Council took responsibility for the remains of the building and an international appeal was launched to achieve re-building.

Re-consecration took place in 1958 and St Clement Danes is now seen as, *'a perpetual shrine of remembrance to those killed on active service and those of the Allied Air Forces who gave their lives during the Second World War, it is a living church prayed in daily and visited throughout the year by thousands seeking solace and reflection.'*

On 12 March 2013 a Roll of Honour was dedicated at the church which lists members of the Auxiliary Air Force and Royal Auxiliary Air Force who died in service. Amongst those present were HRH the Duke of Gloucester, Patron of the Royal Auxiliary Air Force Foundation and the Chief of the Air Staff, Air Chief Marshal Sir Stephen Dalton.

Speaking at the ceremony, Mark Francois, Minister of State for Defence Personnel, Welfare and Veterans said:

> *'I am privileged to be here today attending this Service of dedication of the Royal Auxiliary Air Force Roll of Honour. The proud history of our Armed Forces is built on its people – the magnificent example of the Royal Auxiliary Air Force is as fine as any in the land – and cannot be forgotten.*
>
> *'Men and women who leave civilian employment to defend the United Kingdom and her interests around the world continue to serve as an inspiration to us all. To read and reflect on the long list of names of those who have fallen in the service of the country is a moving experience. Our growing RAF Reserve Squadrons of today are of equal importance as their forbears, standing shoulder to shoulder with the regular RAF, at home and on our operations overseas.'*

Outside St Clement Danes stand the statues of Air Chief Marshal Lord Dowding and Marshal of the Royal Air Force Sir Arthur Harris, who led Bomber Command from 1942 until the end of the war.

The plaque on the Dowding statue reads:

'Air Chief Marshal Lord Dowding was Commander-in-Chief of Fighter Command, Royal Air Force from its formation in 1936 until November 1940. He was thus responsible for the preparation for and the conduct of the Battle of Britain.

'With remarkable foresight, he ensured the equipment of his command with monoplane fighters, the Hurricane and the Spitfire. He was among the first to appreciate the vital importance of R.D.F (Radar) and of an effective command and control system for his squadrons. They were ready when war came.

'In the preliminary stages of that war, he thoroughly trained his minimal forces and conserved them against strong political pressures to disperse and misuse them. His wise and prudent judgement and leadership helped to ensure victory against overwhelming odds and thus prevented the loss of the Battle of Britain and probably the whole war.

'To him the people of Britain and of the free world owe largely the way of life and the liberties they enjoy today.'

Two statues of Air Chief Marshal Sir Keith Park have stood in London in recent years. The first was placed temporarily on a vacant plinth in Trafalgar Square in 2009 and is now in the collection of the RAF Museum. The second was unveiled in Waterloo Place, not far from Trafalgar Square, in 2010. The campaign for a statue of Sir Keith in London was led by businessman Terry Smith. A bust at the National Memorial to The Few at Capel-le-Ferne also pays tribute to Sir Keith. The Duchess of Cornwall unveiled the bust in 2010.

Land Presented to the National Trust

Flying Officer Richard Stephen Demetriadi of No 601 (County of London) Squadron was killed in action during the 'Battle of Portland' on 11 August 1940. He was reported to have been last seen pursuing a German aircraft over the Channel, with fuel leaking from his Hurricane. He is buried in Cayeux-sur-Mer Communal Cemetery, France. 'Dick' Demetriadi was the son of Sir Stephen and Lady Demetriadi and his sister was married to Flight Lieutenant William Rhodes-Moorhouse, lost in combat with No 601 Squadron on 6 September 1940.

Sir Stephen (1880–1952), held senior posts concerned with Chambers of Commerce and served on committees, including that, chaired by Lord Bridgeman, which, in 1930, enquired into the administration of the British Legion. Land at Ditchling Beacon, near his Sussex home, was donated to the National Trust by Stephen in memory of Richard. The Beacon is the highest point in East Sussex. A National Trust sign names the donor and the reason for the gift. Both Dick Demetriadi and Willie Rhodes-Moorhouse are commemorated on the war memorial at St Martin's church, Westmeston, Sussex.

A plaque on the cliff at Crackington Haven, North Cornwall explains the area's association with the Battle of Britain. It reads:

'Given to the National Trust in 1959 by Wing Commander A.G. Parnall in memory of his brother Flight Lieutenant Denis Parnall RAF and all who gave their lives in the Battle of Britain 1940.'

Denis Parnall was born in 1915, attended Clifton College and went up to Downing College, Cambridge, where he read Mechanical Sciences. He was a member of the University Air Squadron and served in the Reserve of Air Force Officers, before transferring to the RAFVR in 1938.

Later that year he was granted a permanent commission in the RAF. He held a staff post, then converted to Hurricanes and joined No 249 Squadron at Leconfield at the end of May 1940. He was credited with a share in the destruction of a Junkers Ju 88 on 8 July and went on to achieve more success in the Battle of Britain.

Denis Parnall was promoted to Flight Lieutenant on 3 September and, on 18 September was killed when he was shot down over Gravesend during a patrol. His Hurricane crashed and burned out at Margaretting, Essex. His friend, Pilot Officer (later Wing Commander) John Beazley recalled many years later how he had witnessed Denis Parnall's death.

On his grave in the churchyard of St Gennys near Crackington Haven are the words:

In the memory of
DENIS GEACH PARNALL.
Flight Lieutenant R.A.F. Fighter pilot killed in action in the BATTLE
OF BRITAIN, 18th September 1940 aged 25 years.
PER ARDUA AD ASTRA

The Parnalls had a house nearby. The family owned businesses in Bristol, including George Parnall & Co, which produced a range of machines between the wars, for instance the Parnall Pixie competition aircraft.

Church Memorials

St Margaret's Church, Wrenbury, Cheshire
Sergeant Frederick William Eley is commemorated four times at St Margaret's church, Wrenbury in south Cheshire, in the area where he grew up.

Fred Eley worked for Lloyds Bank before the war and was a member of the RAFVR. In February 1940 he joined No 74 Squadron. He converted to Spitfires at No 6 OTU, Sutton Bridge then rejoined 74 Squadron. He was killed in action on 31 July 1940 when his Spitfire was shot down in flames off Folkestone. The aircraft was pulled ashore and Sergeant Eley's body was recovered. It was brought back to Wrenbury and lies in a family grave in the churchyard, though the headstone shows an inaccurate date of death.

In the church there is a stained glass window listing eight local casualties of the Second World War, including Fred Eley. His name also appears in a book of remembrance and on the stone war memorial in the churchyard.

Extracts from a letter sent by Fred Eley to his sister Molly, dated 11 October 1939 when he was training at Tern Hill, Shropshire:

> 'We fly till it is going dark and in the evening we have to swot. The amazing thing is that we all take it in the right spirit, and although it is a bit tiring we usually find plenty to laugh at. Anyway, it is all for our own good.
>
> 'The flying side of the business is really good. That, we all enjoy. It is not unusual to do five hours in the air in a day. At that rate you can guess we are beginning to feel quite at home in an aeroplane. Once you get the hang of the new machines we have to fly it is quite simple. I have been flying solo for practically three weeks now. By that time one can make the machines do as one likes. A loop becomes just an ordinary thing, the thrill leaves it after a time.'

All Saints Church, Hoby, Leicestershire
The partly 13th century church contains a memorial which reads:

'In loving memory
Of three generations
Annie Mary Beresford 1847–1929
And her son
Hans Aden Beresford MA 1884–1949
26 years Rector of Hoby and Rotherby
And his son
Flt/Lieut Hugh Richard Aden Beresford
1915–1940
Killed in the Battle of Britain
Nil Sine Cruce'

Hugh Beresford joined the RAF on a short service commission in February 1935 and was posted to No 3 Squadron at Port Sudan on 6 March 1936. He returned to the UK with the squadron in August 1936 and then served on the staff of No 1 Anti-Aircraft Co-operation Unit at Biggin Hill. He went on to be appointed Personal Assistant to the then AOC No 11 Group, Air Vice-Marshal Leslie Gossage.

On 14 May 1940 Beresford was posted from No 11 Group. He was briefly attached to the Central Flying School for a refresher course, after which he joined the newly-reformed No 257 Squadron at Hendon, as a Flight Commander, on May 17. In *Finding The Few*, Andy Saunders recounted that he was known as 'Blue Blood' Beresford on the squadron, a reference to his aristocratic looks and bearing.

During the Battle of Britain Beresford was credited with one enemy aircraft destroyed, one probably destroyed and one shared.

In Hurricane P 3049, Beresford was shot down in combat over the Thames Estuary on 7 September 1940. The aircraft crashed at Elmley, Spitend Point, Sheppey, Kent and he was reported 'Missing'. Flight Lieutenant Lance Mitchell of 257 was lost in the same action. Sergeant Hulbert forced landed near Sittingbourne and Sergeant Robinson returned to Debden, his aircraft damaged.

The site of the Beresford crash was excavated in 1971 and further excavation in 1979 found his remains still in the cockpit. Artefacts recovered included the pilot's parachute, which proved to be undamaged.

Flight Lieutenant Beresford was buried at Brookwood Military Cemetery on 16 November 1979 with full military honours. Airmen from The Queen's Colour Squadron and officers from RAF Odiham took part in the ceremony. Squadron Leader the Reverend Roger Huddleston officiated. The excavation and funeral were filmed for a BBC documentary. Air Chief Marshal Sir Christopher Foxley-Norris spoke at the funeral on behalf of the Battle of Britain Fighter Association at a time when the Association was concerned at the way in which some crash site excavations were taking place.

St John the Baptist, Hawkchurch, east Devon

In 1996 a commemorative tablet at this Norman and Early English church was placed to pay tribute to the short life of Sub Lieutenant Henry Greenshields, a Fleet Air Arm officer who lost his life in the Battle of Britain, while serving on attachment with Fighter Command's No 266 Squadron.

Henry Greenshields was born in 1918. He applied to join the RAF before the Second World War but his eyesight was considered inadequate. Instead he joined the RNVR and was called to full-time service in September 1939.

On 17 June 1940 Greenshields was attached to the RAF and sent to No 7 OTU, Hawarden. Having converted to Spitfires, he joined No 266 Squadron at Wittering on 1 July. On 12 August the squadron moved into the front line at Eastchurch and two days later transferred to Hornchurch.

Greenshields probably destroyed a Messerschmitt Bf 110 and damaged two others on 12 August and destroyed a Messerschmitt Bf 109 south-east of Dover on the 15th. The next day he did not return after chasing Bf 109s over the Channel. He was shot down and killed by Leutnant Müller-Duhe. His Spitfire, N 3240, crashed in the suburbs of Calais.

The book *The Battle of Britain Then and Now*, edited by Winston G. Ramsey, quotes from a letter received in the 1970s by the Greenshields family from a French woman who had lived in Calais in 1940 but at the time that she wrote was resident in Canada. In part the letter read:

'On August 16 1940 I witnessed the fight of a British plane with German ones and saw it pass over my house and eventually fall onto the bank of the canal a few hundred yards behind my house. We all ran to this point to see if

we could help in any way but alas there was nothing we could do. To this day I have never forgotten this and I have wanted to write to the parents of this brave young man whose courage in trying to avoid falling on an inhabited area saved so many lives. The Germans, when they removed his body from the plane, presented a guard of honour but we too stood there and prayed very hard for him and thanked him from the very bottom of our hearts for his sacrifice and courage.'

Later in the letter came the words:

'I want to say a very big thank you for your son's courage and ultimate sacrifice and how brave he was in the face of the enemy and how proud you should be to have such a son.'

Greenshields was 22 and is buried in the Calais Southern Cemetery.

All Saints Church, Brenchley, Kent
The church, in a village near Tunbridge Wells, has a history which includes the steeple blowing down in a great storm in 1703. Some of the damage caused was not put right until a restoration scheme for the church was launched at the end of the 20th century.

Many years ago a small plaque was placed in the churchyard wall. It reads:

TO THE UNDYING FAME OF THE
GALLANT LADS WHO FOUGHT
THE BATTLE OF BRITAIN OVER
THIS CORNER OF ENGLAND IN
AUGUST-SEPTEMBER 1940 AND
TO THE GLORIOUS MEMORY OF
THOSE WHO THEN GAVE THEIR LIVES
PER ARDUA AD ASTRA

The American Volunteer Remembered at St Paul's Cathedral
William Meade Lindsley Fiske III was a wealthy American businessman, sportsman and society figure who was born in Chicago in 1911. He had lived in France for a time and studied Economics and History at Trinity Hall, Cambridge. In 1928, aged 16, he had become the youngest, to that point,

gold medalist at the Winter Olympics, as part of the winning American five-man bobsleigh team. At the 1932 Games he carried the American flag at the opening ceremony and gained another gold medal, this time in the four-man bobsleigh event. Billy Fiske also took part in the Le Mans 24 hours motor race, as well as having a reputation for driving very fast on public roads.

In 1938 Billy Fiske married the divorced first wife of the Seventh Earl of Warwick.

In the early days of the Second World War there was official opposition on both sides of the Atlantic to American citizens joining the British forces. The publicity surrounding Fiske led to him being treated as a special case. He was accepted into the RAF on 18 September 1939. He completed his training with an 'above average' rating and joined No 601 (County of London) Squadron, flying Hurricanes from Tangmere, on 13 July 1940. Amongst all the social exclusivity of the pre-war Auxiliary Air Force, 601 Squadron was perhaps the most socially exclusive of all, with its members referring to the squadron as 'The Legion' and outsiders often calling it, 'The Millionaires' Mob' or 'The Millionaires' Squadron'.

Fiske clearly was an exceptional pilot and Group Captain Sir Archibald Hope Bt who commanded 601 Squadron for part of the Battle of Britain was quoted in *The Guardian* in 2002 as saying:

'Unquestionably, Billy Fiske was the best pilot I've ever known. It was unbelievable how good he was. He picked it up so fast it wasn't true. He'd flown a bit before, but he was a natural fighter pilot. He was also terribly nice and extraordinarily modest, and fitted into the squadron very well.'

Pilot Officer Fiske's aircraft was set on fire during combat on 16 August. He did not bale out but forced landed on the airfield at Tangmere while it was being bombed. Groundcrew pulled him from the burning aircraft and he was taken to hospital, where for a time he seemed to be recovering from his serious burns. However, he died suddenly on 17 August. He was buried in St Mary and St Blaise churcyard at Boxgrove Priory, close to Tangmere.

On 4 July 1941, American Independence Day, a bronze memorial plaque was unveiled in St Paul's Cathedral, at a time when bringing the United States into the war was a key part of British policy.

The plaque read: *'Pilot Officer William Meade Lindsley Fiske III, Royal Air Force, An American Citizen who died that England Might Live. Per Ardua ad Astra'"*

As he revealed the plaque, Sir Archibald Sinclair, Secretary of State for Air, remarked: *'Here was a young man for whom life held much. Under no kind of compulsion he came to fight for Britain. He came and he fought and he died.'*

Billy Fiske is also remembered at Boxgrove Priory. A stained glass window in his memory was unveiled in 2008, having been commissioned by the Old Comrades Association of No 601 Squadron.

Christ Church, Perth, Western Australia

Across the world a window at Christ Church, Claremont, Perth, Western Australia, commemorates local man, Flying Officer Richard Lindsay 'Dick' Glyde, lost in action over the Channel in a Hurricane of No 87 Squadron on 13 August 1940.

In her book *Defending Britain*, Kristen Alexander wrote:

'[Dick Glyde's parents]: *commissioned a stained glass window to replace a window on the north side of the church. Its iconography reveals how the Glydes viewed their son's life, service and death. The Lamb of God represents a willing sacrifice, indicating that they recognised Dick's death as a sacrifice within the Christian tradition of battle against evil. That they perceived their son as a chivalrous knight of the air is demonstrated by the inclusion of two patron saints of chivalry, the archangel Michael and Saint George. At the bottom of the window is the RAF badge, its spreading eagle wings iconographically linking it to St Michael's wings and representing Dick's passion for service flying. The Glyde Window was dedicated at Evensong on 15 December 1946. 470 people attended, including the window's benefactors, Phillis and Frank Glyde, who was in his final illness. Frail and weak, but it isn't hard to imagine the pride and joy, intermingled with renewed grief, that he felt in being able to witness the dedication of the remembrance window.'*

Stanley Cathedral, Falkland Islands

The Cathedral has a plaque in memory of Flight Lieutenant Donald Eric Turner of No 238 Squadron who was shot down and killed over Convoy Peewit on August 8 1940. He had been born in Stanley on 31 July 1910.

'Aerodrome Churches'

Churchyards close to airfields have been designated for the burial of personnel from the airfields concerned, or have naturally performed that function.

An example is the 700-year-old Holy Trinity church at Warmwell, Dorset, close to the former Warmwell airfield, part of No 10 Group in 1940. The Dorset Historic Churches Trust notes that:

> 'Externally, the view of the building must be almost unique in that the chancel is considerably taller than the nave, suggesting some dramatic alterations during its lifetime. The nave is Early English (1200–1300), but was obviously restored about 1450 because the windows belong to the perpendicular period (1401–1500). The tower was added later at about 1600 by the simple expedient of erecting it against the west wall of the church. Two Cinquefoil windows can still be seen that would have once lit the western end of the church.
>
> 'At the opposite end of the building a Victorian chancel of 1881 has been grafted on. It was designed by R C Bennett of Weymouth and physically constructed by the incumbent, the Rev Edward Pickard-Cambridge assisted by his gardener Charles Bushrod and two village masons.'

Six pilots killed during the Battle of Britain are buried at Warmwell, the graves all being together.

They are Pilot Officer Harold Akroyd (No 152 Squadron), Sergeant Alan Feary (No 609 Squadron), Sergeant Jaroslav Hlavac (Czechoslovakian, Nos 79 and 56 Squadrons), Flight Lieutenant John Kennedy, (Australian, No 87 Squadron), Squadron Leader Terence Lovell-Gregg (New Zealander, CO of No 87 Squadron) and Sergeant Sidney Wakeling (No 87 Squadron).

'Shuvvel' Lovell-Gregg's Hurricane crashed into a copse at Abbotsbury, Dorset on 15 August 1940. His body with bullet wounds was found by a farmer's son beside the wreckage. Lovell-Gregg was hit when he led a small number of Hurricanes into a German force over Lyme Bay reported as '120 plus hostiles'. He was apparently trying to reach Warmwell when he came down.

An account of Lovell-Gregg's funeral at Warmwell appeared in *Arise to Conquer*, written by 'Widge' Gleed, who was one of No 87 Squadron's flight commanders and became acting CO on Lovell-Gregg's death.

Gleed wrote that, '*the world seemed too beautiful for a funeral.*' There were three mourners at the graveside, all pilots from the squadron who had flown from Exeter where they were stationed. There were also three wreaths, one from 87 Squadron, one from RAF Exeter and one from RAF Warmwell.

St Luke's Church, Whyteleafe, Surrey is situated not far from Kenley airfield. A corner of the churchyard has been known for many years as 'Airmen's Corner'. Buried there are thirteen RAF aircrew and groundcrew who died during the Battle of Britain.

Among them, and a long way from home, is Pilot Officer Kirkpatrick MacLure Sclanders, one of the considerable Canadian contingent on No 242 Squadron. He had been born in Saskatoon, Saskatchewan in 1916 but had grown up in St John, New Brunswick. He learned to fly in his teens and acted at air shows as a boy scout who accidentally started an aircraft's engine, before performing aerobatics.

Sclanders joined the RAF on a short service commission in 1935, ill health caused him to leave the RAF in 1937 and he returned to Canada. He worked as a journalist and was unsuccessful in an attempt to join the Royal Canadian Air Force. He hoped to fly for Finland against the Russians, but that conflict came to an end and Sclanders travelled to France, hoping to join that country's Air Force. When France collapsed he managed to get to England by ship, where he resumed his RAF career. He coverted to Hurricanes at the operational training unit at Sutton Bridge on the Lincolnshire/Norfolk/Cambridgeshire borders.

On 26 August 1940 Pilot Officer Sclanders was posted to No 242 Squadron at Coltishall. His operational career would last two weeks. On 9 September he was shot down and killed whilst in combat with Messerschmitt Bf 110s and Dornier Do 17s over the Thameshaven oil refinery. His Hurricane fell at Marden Park Farm, Caterham, Surrey.

St Luke's church itself suffered during the Battle of Britain and claims to be the first English church to be damaged by enemy action during the Second World War. On 13 August a bomb intended for Kenley fell between the church and Whyteleafe Hill. All the windows in the north wall were shattered and later replaced. Fragments of glass were collected from those destroyed and turned into a new window.

A Battle of Britain Clasp holder who survived the war, but is buried with his comrades at St Luke's is Air Commodore Roy Gilbert Dutton who died in 1988.

Dutton was born in Ceylon in 1917, joining the RAF on a short service commission in 1936. He became an ace in the Battle of France as a Flight Commander with No 145 Squadron. He was awarded the DFC, going on to further success in the Battle of Britain and the awarding of a bar to the DFC.

He led No 512, a Dakota squadron, during the Rhine Crossing in 1945 and received the DSO. He was later made CBE and retired from the RAF in 1970.

On the north wall of the nave of the church is a Book of Remembrance containing the names of RAF personnel from Kenley who lost their lives during the Battle of Britain.

The Locomotives

In 1941 the Southern Railway introduced a class of express steam locomotives designed by the company's Chief Mechanical Engineer, Oliver Bulleid. There were various unusual, even controversial, features of these locomotives, including an 'air-smoothed' casing which gave them a distinctive appearance.

The original intention was that members of the class would feature the names of British land, sea and air victories of the war then in progress. A wooden test nameplate was prepared carrying the words The Plate, intended to commemorate the Battle of the River Plate in December 1939 which resulted in the scuttling of the German 'pocket Battleship', *Admiral Graf Spee*.

Eventually it was concluded that there were not sufficient victories at that stage of the war. Royal Navy and Commonwealth capital ships were considered as a subject, before it was decided that the new locomotives should become the Merchant Navy class, with each member carrying the name of a shipping company that had used the port of Southampton before the war.

In 1945 a smaller version of the design, known as the West Country class, began entering service. These were named after cities, towns and other geographical locations in the west of England. Eventually the names proposed were becoming obscure and a significant number of the locomotives were operating in south-east England. It was therefore decided that some would be named to commemorate the RAF achievement in the Battle of Britain and would be known as the Battle of Britain class, although there were no design changes to differentiate these locomotives from the West Country class.

Eventually there were forty-four Battle of Britain locomotives, many named after squadrons and airfields associated with the battle, as well as personalities

– Winston Churchill, Lord Dowding, Sir Keith Park, Sir Trafford Leigh-Mallory, Sir Frederick Pile, Sir Archibald Sinclair, Lord Beaverbrook. There were locomotives named, 'Fighter Command', 'Fighter Pilot', 'Anti Aircraft Command' and 'Royal Observer Corps', and one given the somewhat clumsy appellation, 'Sir Eustace Missenden Southern Railway', in tribute both to the company's General Manager and the considerable part played by the Southern in the war effort.

Most Battle of Britain engines carried the appropriate squadron badge or other devices. Eastleigh works mistakenly placed Sir Frederick Pile's coat of arms on 'Kenley' and the RAF badge intended for Kenley on 'Sir Frederick Pile'. The mistake was never corrected. Other devices included a Royal Observer Corps long service award on that locomotive. In addition to an RAF badge, 'Tangmere' displayed station badges donated by the sergeants' mess at Tangmere.

There were naming ceremonies for some locomotives. For example, at Brighton station on 19 September 1947 Air Chief Marshal Sir Keith Park named 'his' locomotive and two officers who had earned the Battle of Britain Clasp, Group Captain D.R.S. Bader and Wing Commander W.G. Clouston, performed the ceremonies for, respectively, 'Fighter Pilot' and 'Tangmere'.

Some Battle of Britain locomotives were later rebuilt without their air-smoothed casings.

On 30 January 1965 'Winston Churchill' (Driver Alf Hurley and Fireman Jim Lester) headed the funeral train of the former Prime Minister from Waterloo station in London to Handborough in Oxfordshire, for his burial at Bladon. There were two standby engines available, 'Biggin Hill' at Nine Elms locomotive shed, Battersea and 'Fighter Command' at Staines Central.

The last examples of the class in main line service were withdrawn in 1967. A number have been preserved including 'Winston Churchill' in the national collection at York and 'Sir Keith Park' which was restored from scrapyard condition over twelve years and entered service on the Severn Valley Railway in 2012.

Royal Observer Corps Memorial

The Observer Corps, as it was titled in 1940, played a major part in the detection and reporting of enemy aircraft during the Battle of Britain. Its origins can be traced back to the work, during and after the Great War, by

Major General Edward Ashmore to defend London against actual and potential air attacks.

In 1924 Ashmore organised trials, using the area between Romney Marsh and Tonbridge. Observer Corps groups were formed in 1925, one with its headquarters at Maidstone and the other based at Tonbridge.

After this, there was steady development. As the website of the Royal Observer Corps Association explains:

> 'On 1 January 1929, control was handed over to the Air Ministry and the Observer Corps headquarters established in Hillingdon House, RAF Uxbridge. The Observer Corps was now a corporate body and it was logical therefore that it should be given an officer in command. The AOC-in-C Air Defence of Great Britain made the suggestion in a letter to the Air Ministry, that an officer of the rank of Air Commodore or Group Captain on the retired list should be appointed the first Commandant of the Observer Corps. As Commandant of the Corps, he would carry out his duties directly under the command of Headquarters, Air Defence of Great Britain and would be responsible to the AOC-in-C for the training and maintenance of centres and posts. The Air Ministry agreed, and on the 1 March 1929, appointed Air Commodore E A D Masterman CB CMG CBE AFC RAF (Rtd) as the first Commandant of the Corps. Air Commodore Masterman held his appointment until 1 March 1936, when he retired, he was succeeded by Air Commodore Warrington-Morris CMG OBE RAF (Rtd) who was destined to lead the Corps until well into the Second World War.'

Development continued, sometimes slowly, into the war years. In his despatch on the Battle of Britain in 1941, Air Chief Marshal Dowding pointed out that:

> 'It is important to note that, at this time the Observer Corps constituted the whole means of tracking enemy raids once they had crossed the coastline, their work throughout was quite invaluable, without it, air raid warning systems could not have been operated and inland interceptions would rarely have been made.'

On April 9 1941 it was announced that the King had granted the Observer Corps the title 'Royal'. The ROC's civilian volunteers were stood down in

1995 and headquarters staff based at Bentley Priory were stood down in the following year.

In 2013 a Royal Observer Corps memorial was dedicated at the National Memorial Arboretum at Alrewas, Staffordshire. It is a stone over 6ft tall and carved from a piece of dark grey granite.

BOOKS

Among an enormous number of publications relating to the battle, an example of those that should be particularly studied is:

Men of the Battle of Britain

In 1989 the first edition of *Men of the Battle of Britain* by Kenneth G. Wynn was published. This large volume represented an enormous task of research in an attempt to provide mini biographies, particularly covering service careers, of all the airmen who had qualified for the Battle of Britain Clasp. There were wartime head and shoulders photographs of many of those whose details were included.

A supplementary volume appeared in 1992, which gave updated biographies for some airmen, as well as some newly discovered photographs. There was an updated second edition from a different publisher in 1999.

In 2010 the rights to the book, including to a third edition, were acquired by an anonymous benefactor and immediately donated to the Battle of Britain Memorial Trust. Further research was carried out, with the help of a large number of experts in various fields, in whose number were fluent speakers of relevant languages.

It is expected that this third edition will be published by Frontline and the Memorial Trust in 2015.

Ken Wynn grew up in the London area and served in the RAF in the 1940s. He has lived in New Zealand for many years, making his achievement in producing *Men of the Battle of Britain* all the more remarkable.

Three typical *Men of the Battle of Britain* entries are reproduced here:

JOHN ALBERT AXEL GIBSON

40969 FO Pilot New Zealander 501 Squadron

Gibson was born in Brighton, England on 24 August 1916 and went to New Zealand in 1920. He was educated in Auckland and New Plymouth Boys' High School.

In late 1937 Gibson applied for an RAF short service commission and, after provisional acceptance, sailed for the UK on 7 April 1938 in the RMS *Rangitata*.

He began his flying training at 4 E&RFTS, Brough on 16 May 1938, as a pupil pilot, and on 9 July he went to No 1 RAF Depot, Uxbridge, for an induction course.

He moved on to 3 FTS, South Cerney on 23 July for intermediate and advanced training. With the course completed, he was posted to No 1 AACU at Farnborough. He later served with 'C' Flight, No 1 AACU, which moved from Weston Zoyland to Penrhos on 4 December 1939. On this day Gibson was attached to 9 Air Observer School.

He was posted from 'C' Flight, No 1 AACU to No 1 RAF Depot at Uxbridge on 20 May 1940, for onward movement to France.

Gibson joined 501 Squadron at Anglure on 21 May. He destroyed a He 111 and shared a second on 27 May, during which action he was shot down, crash-landing in a field. On the 29th he got a probable He 111, on the 30th shot down a He 111 and damaged another, on 4 June damaged another and on the 5th probably destroyed a He 111 and damaged another.

On the 10th Gibson destroyed a Bf 109 but was himself shot down and baled out near Le Mans. His final success in France was a Bf 109, possibly shot down on the 14th. No 501 Squadron was withdrawn from France on 18 June, operated from Jersey on the 19th and re-assembled at Croydon on 21 June.

Gibson claimed a He 111 damaged on 9 July, a Do 17 destroyed on the 13th, a Ju 87 destroyed and another damaged on the 29th and a Do 17 damaged on the 31st. He destroyed a Ju 87, damaged another and destroyed a Bf 109 on 12 August. When he landed back at Hawkinge, Gibson tipped up his Hurricane, P 2986, into a bomb crater.

On the 15th he shot down a Ju 87 and damaged another. In this action, Gibson's Hurricane, P 3582, was set alight by return fire. He steered it away from Folkestone, bringing it down to 1,000 feet before baling out.

On 24 August Gibson destroyed a Ju 88. On 25 August he was appointed 'A' Flight Commander and promoted to Acting Flight Lieutenant next day. On the 28th he damaged a Bf 109 and on the 29th he shot down a Bf 109. In this combat he was again set on fire and baled out over the sea, two miles offshore, and was picked up by a motor boat. Gibson was awarded the DFC (30.8.40).

He damaged a Do 17 on 2 September, shot down a Bf 109 on the 6th and damaged another on the 7th. His last operational sortie with 501 was on 23 September. The following day he evidently became ill and was admitted to Princess Mary's RAF Hospital at Halton. He was posted away from 501 on 2 October 1940.

Gibson joined 53 OTU, Heston on 28 May 1941, as an instructor. In early January 1942 he went to 457(RAAF) Squadron at Jurby, as a Flight Commander. On the expiry of his short service commission, he returned to New Zealand in May 1942 and was attached to the RNZAF from 13 June.

Gibson joined the newly-formed 15 Squadron and went with it to Tonga, where it took over the P 40s of the 68th Pursuit Squadron, USAAF, with which aircraft it eventually became operational.

Gibson returned to New Zealand in mid-December 1942, to a staff job at Air HQ Control Group. In May 1943 he went on a course at the Army Staff College at Palmerston North. On 15 December he returned to 15 Squadron, this time as CO.

The squadron took part in the heavy fighting of the Bougainville landings. Gibson destroyed a Zeke fighter on 23 January 1944. The squadron returned to New Zealand for a rest on 11 February and returned to Guadalcanal in May 1944, moving in June to Bougainville. Tour-expired, Gibson returned with the squadron to New Zealand in late July and was posted away in August. He left for the UK on 31 October 1944.

Gibson flew with 80 Squadron at Volkel from 3 March to 2 April 2 1945 and was involved in the Rhine crossing, covering the airborne operation. He was awarded the DSO (11.3.45). On 1 December 1945 he ceased his attachment to the RAF and transferred to the RNZAF but on 24 December 1946 he rejoined the RAF.

In 1947 Gibson was pilot of Montgomery's personal aircraft, in 1948/49 he was personal aide and pilot to Marshal of the RAF Lord Tedder. He retired from the RAF in 1954 and went to live in South Africa, where he flew for the Chamber of Mines in Johannesburg.

Gibson later moved to their forward base in Bechuanaland, where he operated nine DC 3s and four DC 4s, both as CFI and until 1965 as a Line Captain. He then formed Bechuanaland National Airways and was its General Manager.

In 1969/70 Gibson took part in 'sanction-busting' after UDI in Rhodesia. He flew supplies in and brought refugee children out of Biafra during the war there. On these flights his son, Michael, flew as co-pilot. Gibson later formed an air charter company, Jagair, operating from Kariba, Zimbabwe.

He retired in 1982 and returned to the UK in 1987. Gibson died in July 2000.

APO 9.7.38 PO 16.5.39 FO 3.9.40 FL 3.9.41 SL 1.7.44 FL 1.12.42

GEORGE ERNEST GOODMAN
42598 PO Pilot British 1 Squadron

Goodman was born in Haifa, Palestine on 8 October 1920, the son of a British official of Palestine Railways. He was a boarder, at Highgate School, London. Goodman was a member of the OTC there.

It was thought that he would go to University but when his father left Palestine to go on to Nigeria, Goodman accompanied him to England, to join the RAF on a short service commission.

He began his *ab initio* course at 11 E&RFTS, Perth on 10 July 1939, moved to 9 FTS, Hullavington on 2 September and on to 15 FTS, Lossiemouth on the 23rd, successfully completing the course there on 17 February 1940.

Goodman was posted to 11 Group Pool at St Athan on the 27th, went to Sutton Bridge on 9 March, when 11 Group Pool was redesignated 6 OTU. After converting to Hurricanes, he joined No 1 Squadron at Vassincourt, France on 1 May 1940.

South of Rheims on 14 May, Goodman shared in the destruction of a He 111, with Flight Lieutenant PP Hanks. On 17 June Goodman was credited with a He 111 (actually a Ju 88). The squadron was withdrawn to Northolt the next day.

On 25 July Goodman was attacked by four Bf 109s off Portland and did not fire his guns but one of the 109s spun into the sea after a violent breakaway. He shared in the destruction of a Do 17 off Cherbourg on 11 August, destroyed a He 111 on the 16th and shared a Do 17 and destroyed a Bf 110 and shared a Do 17 on the 18th. Whilst shooting the Bf 110 down, Goodman was attacked by a Bf 109, which chased him back to the English coast, filling his Hurricane with cannon shells and bullets. Goodman landed safely but his aircraft was a write-off.

During a big raid on London on 6 September, Goodman shot down a Bf 110 and was himself shot down in flames by return fire. He baled out, with a sprained shoulder. His Hurricane, P 2686, crashed at Brownings Farm, Chiddingstone Causeway. Goodman flew again two days later.

He shared a Ju 88 on 8 October, damaged a Do 17 attacking RAF Feltwell on the 27th, which escaped into cloud and regained its base with crew wounded, and on the 30th he shared in the destruction of a Ju 88. He was awarded the DFC (26.11.40).

Goodman was with 73 Squadron at Castle Camps by 9 November 1940. On the 10th he embarked on HMS *Furious* with the squadron, bound for the Middle East. He flew Hurricane V 7535 off to Takoradi on 29 November, to fly the ferry route north to Heliopolis, via Lagos, Accra, Kano, Maiduguri, Khartoum, Wadi Halfa and Abu Sueir.

At Lagos on 5 December 1940 Goodman saw his mother, for what was to be the last time. He missed seeing his father, who was away with an economic mission in the Belgian Congo. When No 73 left Lagos, their Hurricanes did a roll over the Goodman home at Ebutte Metta and were gone.

During December the pilots of 73 were attached to 274 Squadron in the Western Desert. The squadron became operational again, as a unit, in early January 1941. On 4 February Goodman shot down a CR 42 in flames near Benina aerodrome and on 9 April destroyed a Bf 110 near Tobruk. In this engagement Goodman was himself shot down by Bf 110s and crash-landed behind British lines. On the 14th he shared in the destruction of a Hs 126 and on the 21st destroyed a Ju 87 over Tobruk and shared a second.

In late March/early April Goodman had spent a short leave in Haifa with his two sisters and took his friend Flying Officer O.E. Lamb with him. On 14 April, the day Lamb was killed, Goodman shared a Hs 126. On the 21st he destroyed a Ju 87 over Torbruk and shared a second.

Goodman destroyed a Fiat G-50 on 22 April and on 23 May he damaged a Ju 88 over Crete. He was shot down and killed on 14 June 1941. Six aircraft, led by Goodman, were making a strafing attack on Gazala airfield. Heavy flak was encountered and three of the Hurricanes were lost in the operation.

One of the other aircraft lost was piloted by Sergeant John White DFM, who had flown with 72 Squadron in the Battle of Britain. Goodman is buried in Knightsbridge War Cemetery, Acroma, Libya.

APO 2.9.39 PO 28.2.40 FO 28.2.41

PETER HOWES
74332 PO Pilot British 54 and 603 Squadrons

Howes, of Wadebridge, Cornwall, was educated at Oundle School and St John's College, Oxford, where he read Natural Science. He learned to fly with the University Air Squadron and he was a friend of Richard Hillary.

In June 1939 Howes joined the RAFVR, as an Airman u/t Pilot (754281). He was called up on 1 September and commissioned on the 26th.

Howes completed his training at 14 FTS, Kinloss on No 4 Course, which ran from 20 November 1939 to 11 May 1940. On completion, he was posted to No 1 School of Army Co-operation at Old Sarum for No 1 Course, from 20 May to 22 June.

On the 23rd Howes was sent to 5 OTU, Aston Down and after converting to Spitfires, he joined 54 Squadron at Rochford on 8 July. He moved to 603 Squadron at Hornchurch on 10 September.

Howes was shot down and killed by Bf 109s on the 18th. His Spitfire, X 4323, crashed at Kennington, near Ashford. Howes was 21. He was cremated at St John's Crematorium, Woking.

School Plaques

In recent years a considerable variety of schools in the UK and beyond have put in place plaques commemorating former pupils who flew in the Battle of Britain. Some of these have been provided by the schools or people associated with them, while others have been inspired by the Battle of Britain Historical Society or other bodies.

Some examples are:

At **Malvern College** in Worcestershire a plaque was placed in 2010 listing those old boys of the school who qualified for the Battle of Britain Clasp. As more information came to light the plaque was added to.

Those commemorated are:

D.L. Armitage	H.A.V Hogan
C.C.M. Baker	R.H. Holland
A.W.A. Bayne	G.C.M. Peters
G.W. Cory	W.H. Warner
D. Crowley-Milling	B.H. Way
R.A.L. Du Vivier	

In 2011 a plaque was unveiled at **Coleg Sir Gar (Carmarthenshire College)**, the successor establishment to Llanelli Boys' Grammar School. The plaque, initiated by the Battle of Britain Historical Society, honoured an old boy of the Grammar School, Sergeant Lewis Reginald 'Reg' Isaac and was unveiled by Lord Howard of Lympne, former Leader of the Conservative Party, who had also attended the school.

Sergeant Isaac had been a pre-war member of the RAFVR. He completed his training in the first months of the war and on 27 July 1940 joined No 64 Squadron.

Nine days later he was shot over the Channel during his first operational sortie. Spitfires from the squadron were bounced (taken by surprise) by Messerschmitt Bf 109s during a dawn patrol. Sergeant Isaac's aircraft, L 1029, fell into the water. His body was not recovered so his name appears on the Runnymede Memorial.

Former Warrant Officer H.D. 'Dave' Denchfield flew in the latter stages of the Battle of Britain with No 610 Squadron. He was honoured by his old school in Hertfordshire in 2011, not long before he died.

After the ceremony his son Nigel wrote:

'The **Hemel Hempstead School** opened in 1931, and my father won a place there as part of the first intake of 50. It converted to a comprehensive in the 70s, but it still runs in a very traditional way, and clearly honours its past. In October 2011 they had a day to celebrate the 80th anniversary (of the school), and chose that day to unveil the Battle of Britain Historical Society plaque that we had already initiated. This served a very useful purpose as they were keen to have my father at the 80th birthday, so we only had to journey there once!

'It was fairly low key ceremony, the Head spoke well of the deeds and sacrifice of the RAF pilots and my father made one of his off the cuff replies that amused them at times.

'They then had a session on a memorial bench to the school as a whole, with my father, another chap called Cyril Lewis from the next intake, and the two youngest pupils in the school ... a pair of 6th form girls then interviewed my father for about 45 minutes as part of a research project they were carrying out. This was not part of their studies, but something they were genuinely interested in, we were most impressed.'

David Denchfield was shot down in February 1941, during a Blenheim escort sortie over France, and spent the rest of the war as a prisoner. He died in 2012.

Another occasion on which the Battle of Britain Historical Society took the initiative was in 2011 at **Rendcomb College**, Gloucestershire, when the person honoured was Squadron Leader Vernon Douglas 'Doug' Page who had flown with No 610 Squadron in 1940 and who died in 2001. The ceremony was part of the annual Old Rendcombians Day.

In part the plaque remembering Doug Page reads:

'His participation in the Battle of Britain in 1940 helped to prevent an invasion of this country and the subjugation of its people.'

The 610 (County of Chester) Squadron Association was instrumental, when, in 2011, a plaque was unveiled at **St John Plessington Catholic College**, at Bebington on the Wirral, in memory of Squadron Leader C.S. 'Bam' Bamberger, who had died in 2008. His widow and sons were present and a service was conducted by the school chaplain.

School plaques exist overseas too. In 2011 an unveiling took place at **The Hutchins School** in Hobart, Tasmania, with the airmen and former pupil honoured being Flight Lieutenant Stuart Crosby Walch of No 238 Squadron, lost in the 'Battle of Portland' on 11 August 1940, flying from Middle Wallop.

Kristen Alexander, historian and author, who initiated the ceremony on behalf of the Battle of Britain Historical Society wrote in *1940* magazine:

'Stuart flew just over 50 operational sorties with No 238 Squadron. He was one of the first Australians to score a victory against the enemy during the Battle of Britain and accounted for two enemy aircraft destroyed, two shared, one unconfirmed shared and one damaged.

'Although only 23, he was known as the father of his squadron. He had a reputation of taking on the most dangerous jobs himself and shepherding young pilots so they could make their first 'kills' safely. But on August 11 1940 he was caught between two waves of enemy aircraft. He did not baulk at the overwhelming numbers but led his flight into the onslaught. Stuart battled bravely but he and his section plummeted into the water five miles or so south of Swanage.

'From the same engagement, Sergeant Gledhill, Pilot Officer Cawse and Flying Officer Steborowski failed to return.'

At the ceremony at The Hutchins School Air Vice-Marshal Mark Skidmore. Air Commander Australia, declared that, *'Stuart may have been an RAF man when he died but he was an RAAF man at heart. He is well remembered. The Hutchins School honours him as an inspiration and example. I, and the Royal Australian Air Force, honour Stuart Crosby Walch as one of our own.'*

Other Memorials

Duxford
RAF Duxford, Cambridgeshire was a sector station in No 12 Group during the Battle of Britain. The RAF left in 1961. In 1968 scenes for the film *Battle of Britain* were filmed there.

Now the airfield is a station of the Imperial War Museums and a major base for historic aircraft, both on display and capable of flying. Among the many exhibitions is one dedicated to the Battle of Britain, located in hangar 4.

Benzie Lake
Benzie Lake in Manitoba, Canada was given that name in 1953 in honour of Pilot Officer John 'Jack' Benzie of No 242 Squadron, who failed to return from a combat over the Thames Estuary on 7 September 1940, aged 25.

Jack Benzie came from Winnipeg and had served in Princess Patricia's Canadian Light Infantry before joining the RAF on a short service commission. He was shot down in both the Battle of France and the Battle of Britain. On 23 May 1940 he baled out, wounded, south of Dunkirk and escaped by sea to England.

His final combat came on the day of the first massive German raid on London. At the time Benzie was reported as missing. It is strongly believed that his remains and those of his Hurricane were found in 1976 when a site was excavated in a field between Theydon Bois and Loughton in Essex. However, the evidence was considered insufficient and the remains were buried at Brookwood Military Cemetery as those of an unknown airman. Benzie's name appears on the Runnymede Memorial.

Salem-Leckrone Airport
Another very large tribute to one of The Few in North America is Salem-Leckrone Airport at Salem, Illinois, perpetuating the memory of Pilot Officer Phillip Howard 'Uncle Sam' Leckrone, one of the Americans who

volunteered for the RAF. Leckrone came from Salem and was a civilian pilot before the war. He served with No 616 Squadron from 2 September and 12 October 1940, when he was posted to No 71 Squadron, then forming as the first 'Eagle' squadron with American volunteers. Leckrone would become the squadron's first fatality when he died as a result of a mid-air collision during a formation practice on 5 January 1941.

The Lewis Chain, Antarctica

There is a geographical feature in Antarctica that commemorates a Battle of Britain airman. The Lewis Chain of rocky features, west of the Gordon Glacier in the Shackleton range, recalls Group Captain John Harding Lewis (1922–1990). As a Squadron Leader he was leader of the RAF contingent with the Commonwealth Trans-Antarctic expedition led by Vivian Fuchs. The naming recognised the outstanding contribution of Lewis to the expedition, including the fact that he became the first person to make a trans-Antarctic flight in a single-engined aircraft. Lewis (who also received the AFC and bar during his career) was awarded the Polar Medal and Fuchs was knighted.

In the Battle of Britain LAC Lewis had been a Radar Operator with No 25 Squadron and had flown two operational sorties. He went on to qualify as a pilot.

Public Houses

Some public houses have names linked to the battle. They include **The Bader Arms** in the village of Tangmere, West Sussex, near the former airfield. It is named in tribute to Group Captain Sir Douglas Bader (1910–1982), who, as a Squadron Leader, commanded No 242 Squadron in the battle, despite the loss of both his legs as a result of a pre-war flying accident.

There is also **The Douglas Bader** pub and restaurant at Martlesham Heath in Suffolk, a village which also gave its name to a Battle of Britain airfield.

Another example of a pub with a Battle of Britain association is **The Shepley Spitfire** at Totley, near Sheffield, named in honour of Pilot Officer Douglas Shepley, killed in action in the battle, and the aircraft that later carried his name. The Shepley family lived at Woodthorpe Hall close to where the pub now stands.

Just before the war Douglas Shepley was an officer cadet at Cranwell, where he demonstrated that he was an outstanding sportsman. The records there show that he represented the College at Rugby Union, Athletics and Boxing.

Early in the war he lost two of his siblings. His sister Jeanne, a Volunteer in the Women's Transport Service, had died on 18 October 1939 when the SS *Yorkshire* of the Bibby Line, sailing from Rangoon to Liverpool, was torpedoed and sunk about 800 miles west of Bordeaux. The ship was part of convoy HG3 and the attack was carried out by U-boat, U-37. There were 220 survivors, picked up by the American vessel, *Independence Hall* and 58 people were lost.

Beyond the Call of Duty by Brian James Crabb records that the *Independence Hall* had already saved survivors from the *City of Mandalay*, part of the same convoy and sunk by U-46. While the rescue of passengers and crew from Yorkshire was taking place, a U-boat surfaced and a voice, speaking good English, thanked Captain Mackenzie of the *Independence Hall* for what he was doing.

On 31 May 1940, Flight Lieutenant George Rex Shepley was the pilot of a Lysander of No 16 Squadron shot down over Dunkirk while on a tactical reconnaissance sortie. G.R. Shepley was reported killed and Pilot Officer Hare missing.

Flight Lieutenant Shepley had been previously wounded on 27 May. His Lysander was badly damaged by AA fire on an early morning supply mission to Calais and crashed on return to Lympne. The other crew member, Corporal Jones, was also wounded. The crew had flown this sortie not knowing that Calais had already fallen to German troops.

Douglas Shepley had joined No 152 Squadron at Acklington, Northumberland.

On 12 July 1940, 152 Squadron moved to Warmwell in Dorset, in the Middle Wallop sector of No 12 Group. A key task allocated to the squadron was the defence of the Portland naval base.

August 12 was the day before the launch of Operation Adlerangriff, the German all-out assault on Fighter Command. About 12.20pm two 152 Spitfires were shot down south of the Isle of Wight. One was flown by Douglas Shepley and the other by Flight Lieutenant Carr Withall, from Australia. Neither body was found and the names of both officers appear on the Runnymede Memorial.

Douglas Shepley had married six weeks before his death. His widow, Frances, and his mother, Emily, set out to raise the money to replace the Spitfire that Douglas had been flying.

They gained the support of Lord Beaverbook, Minister of Aircraft Production and, helped by collections in all the ARP posts in Sheffield, £5,700 was raised in less than four months.

When he received the money, Lord Beaverbrook sent Mrs Shepley senior a letter of thanks in which he wrote:

'Will you allow me in sending you my heartfelt sympathy in the tragic losses you have sustained, to tell you how proud I am convinced your sons and daughter would be to know of the tribute you have paid in their memory.'

On 16 August 1941 The Shepley Spitfire was issued to No 602 (City of Glasgow) Squadron. It was lost on 28 March 1942 while being flown by Group Captain Victor Beamish, a Battle of Britain veteran.

The pub in Totley opened in 1979 and the first pint was pulled by Seymour, one of a total of five brothers, together with Rex, Frank, Douglas and Peter. The Shepley family continued to live at Woodthorpe Hall and to hold Rex's DFC.

As a last instance of this form of commemoration, **The Battle of Britain** pub can be found in Coldharbour Road, Northfleet, near Gravesend, Kent.

Family Memorials

An instance of a memorial to Battle of Britain airman created by the family is the sundial in the churchyard at Holy Trinity, Great Paxton, Huntingdonshire. This marks the grave of Pilot Officer Philip Melville 'Pip' Cardell, No 603 Squadron, who was killed during the heavy fighting on 27 September 1940.

In 1939 Philip Cardell had worked to improve the garden of the family home next to the church, constructing a pond and adding a sundial as part of the process. The sundial was moved into the churchyard to mark his grave. Originally the accompanying plaque gave an incorrect date of death, but this has now been corrected.

The circumstances of Philip Cardell's loss were also somewhat unusual. His Spitfire was badly damaged during combat over the Channel, he baled out off Folkestone, but his parachute failed to open. Pilot Officer Peter Dexter, also of 603, witnessed what had happened, landed his aircraft on the beach and reached Cardell in a rowing boat, only to have to bring his body ashore.

RAF Uxbridge

Down seventy-six steps at the former RAF Uxbridge, is the No 11 Group bunker. Here is housed what from 1939 to 1958 was the Group's ops room. Originally operations were controlled from an adjacent building, but with war ever more likely, the decision was taken to create a new operations room underground. It was ready for use in late August 1939. Here, and at his nearby office in Hillingdon House, Air Vice-Marshal Keith Park took many of the key decisions of the battle.

Today the bunker and its associated museum is regarded, according to the service's website, as *'the Royal Air Force's primary Force Development and Public Engagement asset'*. It comes under the auspices of the Squadron Leader who serves as Media & Communications Officer, based at RAF Northolt. There is a post of Curator for the bunker, vacant at the time this was written, and a Friends of the No 11 Group Operations Rooms organization, founded in 2010. This body raises funds, promotes visits to the bunker and provides volunteer guides.

After use for signals and communication purposes, the bunker was restored to its wartime condition in 1975. Much development work and collection of artefacts was carried out after Warrant Officer Chris Wren was given responsibility for the bunker, as a secondary duty. He later continued, as a civil servant, to be the curator, until final retirement. Later curators who contributed to the historic credibility of the bunker were Hazel Crozier and Dan Stirland.

Outside the bunker are replica aircraft and a memorial commemorating all who served with No 11 Group. It was unveiled in 1958 by Lord Dowding.

At Northolt restoration was continuing in 2014 on the Sir Keith Park building, which housed the operations room for Z sector within No 11 Group. As a Group Captain, Keith Park was Northolt Station Commander in 1931–32.

RAF HQ Gibraltar

Until 2013 the headquarters building for the RAF in Gibraltar was named Jaguar House. In that year, the Vice Chief of the Air Staff, Air Chief Marshal Sir Stuart Peach, performed the ceremony in which the HQ was renamed the Rene Mouchotte Building in honour of a distinguished Free French pilot who had qualified for the Battle of Britain Clasp and was killed in action in 1943.

In 1940 Mouchotte was part of a group which had escaped to Gibraltar from Algeria in a stolen aircraft, in order to continue the fight against Nazism after the fall of France.

In his book *The Big Show*, Pierre Clostermann, another outstanding French pilot, wrote of Mouchotte:

> '*A tall, dark, slim man with piercing eyes and a voice that snapped and admitted no argument, but was followed by a warming, friendly smile. The kind of man for whom you get killed, without discussion, almost with pleasure.*'

Present at the re-naming ceremony was the TV personality Jan Leeming who has long campaigned for more recognition for the presence of French airmen amongst those who flew in the Battle of Britain.

There is also a street in Paris named in honour of Rene Mouchotte.

Czechoslovak Memorials
In June 2014 memorials were unveiled in Prague, capital of the Czech Republic and the Slovak capital, Bratislava in memory of Czech and Slovak airmen who served in the RAF in the Second World War. A significant number of those remembered had flown in the Battle of Britain.

Airfield Memorials
Former Battle of Britain airfields that now have memorials to the personnel who served there include, Kenley, Croydon, Hornchurch and North Weald. The Tangmere Military Aviation Museum acts as a memorial to the former personnel of that Battle of Britain sector station.

Road Names
A considerable number of road names pay tribute to the men of the Battle of Britain. Among those with Battle associations are:

Nicolson Drive, Shoreham, Sussex (Flight Lieutenant James Nicolson of No 249 Squadron, who was awarded the Victoria Cross).

Streets built on the former Hawkinge airfield, including Kirton Close, which remembers Sergeant David Kirton, RAFVR, who was killed in action as a Spitfire pilot with No 65 Squadron on 8 August 1940.

Roads in the former married quarters at Biggin Hill recall the three WAAFs who earned the Military Medal at the station during the battle.

On 14 June 2014 a road in the Jersey parish of St Ouen was named Rue Henri Gonay, seventy years after Squadron Leader Gonay's death, when his aircraft crashed nearby. At the ceremony his wedding ring – found at the time and kept from the Germans until it could be returned to the family – was worn by Henri Gonay's grandson. Gonay had escaped from Belgium in 1940 and qualified for the Battle of Britain Clasp, flying Blenheims with No 235 Squadron.

RAF VC 10 Aircraft

Some airmen who earned the Victoria Cross were commemorated by the naming of RAF VC 10 transport and air-to-air refuelling aircraft. Among those selected was Flight Lieutenant James 'Nick' Nicolson, the only member of Fighter Command ever to be awarded the VC.

His citation read:

'*Air Ministry, 15 November 1940.*

'*The KING has been graciously pleased to confer the Victoria Cross on the undermentioned officer in recognition of most conspicuous bravery:*

Flight Lieutenant James Brindley NICOLSON (39329) — No. 249 Squadron.

During an engagement with the enemy near Southampton on 16th August 1940, Flight Lieutenant Nicolson's aircraft was hit by four cannon shells, two of which wounded him whilst another set fire to the gravity tank.

When about to abandon his aircraft owing to flames in the cockpit he sighted an enemy fighter. This he attacked and shot down, although as a result of staying in his burning aircraft he sustained serious burns to his hands, face, neck and legs. Flight Lieutenant Nicolson has always displayed great enthusiasm for air fighting and this incident shows that he possesses courage and determination of a high order. By continuing to engage the enemy after he had been wounded and his aircraft set on fire, he displayed exceptional gallantry and disregard for the safety of his own life.'

Nicolson was originally recommended for the DFC for his gallantry. The recommendation that this should be upgraded to the VC came from Air Vice-Marshal Park, commanding No 11 Group.

Other Second World War VCs honoured on VC 10s were Leonard Cheshire, Donald Garland, Guy Gibson, Thomas Gray, David Lord, Hugh Malcolm, George Thompson and Arthur Scarf.

Battle of Britain Tapestry

The idea for a tapestry replicating the window in Westminster Abbey, came from Flight Lieutenant Ron Crook when he was a patient at the RAF Hospital, Halton immediately after the Second World War. At that time, he saw it as occupational therapy for fellow patients. A little work was done, but the project faltered when Flight Lieutenant Crook left hospital.

In the 1980s Ron Crook revived the idea when he was living in Kings Heath, Birmingham and was a member of the local branch of the Royal British Legion. Volunteers came forward and 48 panels were produced containing about 48,000 stitches each. Eleven artists and forty-eight embroiderers had contributed to the finished tapestry. The work was completed for the 50th anniversary of the battle in 1990.

Seven years later Her Majesty Queen Elizabeth the Queen Mother handed the tapestry for safekeeping to the Spitfire and Hurricane Memorial Building at the former Battle of Britain airfield at Manston, Kent.

Film

The film, *Battle of Britain,* was directed by Guy Hamilton, with screenplay by James Kennaway and appeared in 1969. Writing credits were received by Derek Demspster and Derek Wood, authors of the book, *The Narrow Margin.* Clasp holders who acted as key advisers were Group Captain Tom Gleave, Wing Commander Bob Stanford Tuck and Squadron Leader Boleslaw Drobinski. German input came from Leutnant General Adolf Galland.

The film covered the outcome of the Battle of France, the German preparations for invasion as well as representing the aerial fighting over England and the Channel, by means of a large fleet of aircraft specially assembled. There were scenes involving the decision making of Dowding and Park and depictions of the tensions at dispersal points and the impact on London of the start of the Blitz.

At the end of the film pilots sit in their dispersal hut waiting for action that does not come. Nonetheless the strain leads one man to thrust his head out of the door to vomit. At the same time Goering, the Luftwaffe chief, tells senior officers that they have failed him. Air Chief Marshal Dowding leaves his desk at Bentley Priory to stare out of the window at an empty sky. Symbolically the Battle of Britain has been won.

Actual individual Battle of Britain aircrew were not identified in the film. In the order credited the cast was:

Harry Andrews	Senior Civil Servant
Michael Caine	Squadron Leader Canfield
Trevor Howard	Air Vice-Marshal Keith Park
Curd Jürgens	Baron von Richter
Ian McShane	Sgt. Pilot Andy
Kenneth More	Group Capt. Baker
Laurence Olivier	Air Chief Marshal Sir Hugh Dowding
Nigel Patrick	Group Capt. Hope
Christopher Plummer	Squadron Leader Colin Harvey
Michael Redgrave	Air Vice-Marshal Evill
Ralph Richardson	Sir David Kelly, British Minister to Switzerland
Robert Shaw	Squadron Leader Skipper
Patrick Wymark	Air Vice-Marshal Trafford Leigh-Mallory
Susannah York	Section Officer Maggie Harvey
Michael Bates	Warrant Officer Warwick
Robert Flemyng	Wing Cmdr. Willoughby
Isla Blair	Mrs Andy
Barry Foster	Squadron Leader Edwards
John Baskcomb	Farmer (as John Bascomb)
Edward Fox	Pilot Officer Archie
Tom Chatto	Willoughby's Assistant Controller
W.G. Foxley	Squadron Leader Evans
James Cosmo	Jamie
David Griffin	Sgt. Pilot Chris
Jack Gwillim	Senior Air Staff Officer
André Maranne	French NCO (as Andre Maranne)
Myles Hoyle	Peter
Anthony Nicholls	Minister
Duncan Lamont	Flight Sgt. Arthur
Nicholas Pennell	Simon
Sarah Lawson	Skipper's Wife
Andrzej Scibor	Ox

Mark Malicz	Pasco
Jean Wladon	Jean Jacques
Wilfried von Aacken	Gen. Osterkamp (as Wilfried Van Aacken)
Reinhard Horras	Bruno
Karl-Otto Alberty	General Jeschonnek (Luftwaffe Chief of Staff) (as Karl Otto Alberty)
Helmut Kircher	Boehm
Alexander Allerson	Maj. Brandt
Paul Neuhaus	Maj. Föhn
Dietrich Frauboes	Field Marshal Milch (Inspector General, Luftwaffe)
Malte Petzel	Col. Beppo Schmidt (Luftwaffe Intelligence)
Alf Jungermann	Brandt's Navigator
Manfred Reddemann	Maj. Falke
Peter Hager	Field Marshal Albert Kesselring
Hein Riess	Reichsmarschall Hermann Göring
Wolf Harnisch	Gen. Fink (as Wolf Harnish)
Rolf Stiefel	Adolf Hitler

An earlier film depicting the Battle of Britain was *Angels One Five* (1952) in which John Gregson played Pilot Officer 'Septic' Baird, a Battle of Britain Hurricane pilot. Jack Hawkins, Michael Denison and Dulcie Gray were among the other actors to appear. The film's title refers to RAF jargon, 'angels' meaning height in thousands of feet.

National Memorial Aboretum
In June 2014 a tree was planted at the National Memorial Arboretum in Staffordshire on behalf of the Battle of Britain Fighter Association. The accompanying plaque stated that it is, *In memory of all the aircrew who flew, fought and died in the Battle of Britain 10 July–31 October 1940*. Present at the planting were three members of the Association, Flying Officer Ken Wilkinson, Squadron Leader Tony Pickering and Flight Lieutenant Ron Smyth.

Chapter Six

They Have Shaped the BBFA

Here are brief biographies of some of the men who flew in the Battle of Britain and went on to play significant roles in the BBFA.

Air Commodore Peter Malam Brothers CBE DSO DFC and bar

'Pete' Brothers was born in 1917. Having already learned to fly he joined the RAF on a short service commission and began his training in January 1936. He was posted to No 32 Squadron at Biggin Hill, equipped with the Gloster Gauntlet and, in 1938, as Hurricanes arrived, he became a Flight Commander.

During the fighting over France and in the Battle of Britain Brothers quickly became an ace. On 9 September 1940 Brothers was posted, as a Flight Commander to No 257, another Hurricane squadron, then based at Martlesham Heath, Suffolk. Here he worked under the new CO, Squadron Leader Bob Tuck, to revitalise a squadron where morale had sunk very low.

In 1941, after a period instructing and on a course at the Central Flying School, Brothers formed No 457 Squadron, Royal Australian Air Force. In 1942 he commanded No 602 (City of Glasgow) Squadron before taking command of the Tangmere Wing.

In April 1944, after another break from operations, Pete Brothers took command of the Exeter Wing. He decided that to overcome the difficulties of controlling six squadrons spread over a number of airfields, it should be split in two. Brothers commanded what became the Culmhead Wing, with another Battle of Britain veteran, Wing Commander 'Birdie' Bird-Wilson, leading the Harrowbeer Wing.

Brothers was not amongst the Wing leaders, at the time of D-Day, to be awarded the American DFC, because, he said, he declined to fill in his own citation. However, he did go on a course at Fort Levenworth, Kansas. In September 1945 he took part in the first Battle of Britain flypast over London.

After a spell at the Central Fighter Establishment, he left the RAF in 1947, joining the Colonial Service and going to Kenya.

Two years after leaving the service Brothers returned to the RAF. In 1965 he was one of the still serving Battle of Britain Clasp holders selected to march in the funeral procession of Sir Winston Churchill.

Brothers retired from the RAF in 1973. He died in 2008.

Flight Lieutenant John Howard Duart

A varied and colourful life was enjoyed by Howard Duart who was born in Herefordshire in 1905. Between the wars he ran an egg and poultry business before working in Chile and then, for Caribbean Petroleum, in Venezuela. He went on to farm in Sussex. In 1938 he became an articled clerk to a chartered accountant. In the same year he obtained a pilot's licence and in 1939 he joined the Civil Air Guard.

With the declaration of war he volunteered for aircrew duties in the RAF and, in February 1940, he was commissioned as a direct entry air gunner. On 18 March he was posted to No 219 Squadron and flew in Blenheims during the Battle of Britain. He later served in ground roles in the UK and Canada.

He was released from the RAF in 1945 and, three years later, qualified as a chartered accountant.

Howard Duart died in 2007, aged 101.

Wing Commander Robert William Foster DFC AE

Bob Foster was a south Londoner who had a long career before and after the war with Shell and BP. He joined the RAFVR in 1939 to train as a pilot and was called up the day before war broke out.

Foster was commissioned in June 1940, while at No 6 OTU at Sutton Bridge, Lincolnshire. In July he was posted to No 605 (County of Warwick) Squadron, then at Drem, east of Edinburgh. On 7 September, having re-fuelled at Abingdon, so as not to be low on fuel in the area of most action, the squadron arrived at Croydon, as the first large attack on London was taking place.

In later years Bob Foster would recall how the casualties quickly started to mount. On 8 September, over Tunbridge Wells, during an attack on German bombers with fighter escort, Flying Officer John Fleming, a New Zealander, baled out terribly burned. He would become a member of the Guinea Pig Club at East Grinstead. The next day Pilot Officer George Forrester, a keen rugby player and rower, was killed when his Hurricane collided with a Heinkel He lll over Alton, Hampshire.

In combat on 27 September Bob Foster damaged a Messerschmitt Bf 110, but then found that his engine had been hit. He managed to get down in what appeared to be a Sussex field, but was surprised to realise that an RAF 'erk' was standing respectfully beside the aircraft. His answer to the question, *'Where am I?'* was, *'You have landed at RAF Gatwick, sir'*.

Foster made several more claims. He became an instructor in the autumn of 1941 before being appointed a Flight Commander with No 54 Squadron. In 1942 the squadron went to Australia as part of the country's defence against the Japanese, being based first in New South Wales and then at Night Cliff in the Northern Territory. Foster scored more victories and was awarded the DFC on 13 August 1943. He returned to the UK, went with the Air Information Unit to the continent in July 1944, before serving at HQ Fighter Command, Bentley Priory and in ground roles at RAF Bentwaters. He left the RAF in 1947, but later served in the RAuxAF.

Bob Foster died on 30 July 2014. A Hurricane that he had flown in the Battle of Britain passed overhead at his funeral in Hastings.

Group Captain Colin Falkland Gray DSO DFC (and two bars)

Born in Christchurch, New Zealand in 1914, Colin Falkland Gray was accepted for an RAF short service commission in 1938 at the third attempt. His brother Kenneth had been accepted on his first application, the previous year.

C.F. Gray began his RAF training in January 1939. Ten months later he joined a Spitfire squadron, No 54. His first success came on 24 May 1940, when he shared in the destruction of a Messerschmitt Bf 109, but his own aircraft suffered considerable damage. By the time he was awarded the DFC on 15 August he was already an ace and went on to be one of the major RAF scorers of the Battle of Britain. Before the end of 1940 he was posted to No 43 Squadron as a flight commander, then returned to his original squadron in the same capacity.

Gray became a flight commander on No 1 Squadron and was awarded a bar to the DFC in September 1941. After three days in command of No 403 Squadron, he was appointed CO of No 616 Squadron. He later commanded No 64 Squadron and then served in North Africa, including leading No 81 Squadron, a period in which he added significantly to his score. He commanded a Wing in Malta.

An award of the DSO was gazetted on 15 May 1943, with a second bar to the DFC following six months later.

In July 1944 Gray became OC the Detling Wing, moving quickly to the Lympne Wing. He was granted a permanent commission after the war and retired in 1961.

Colin Gray returned to New Zealand and joined Unilever, retiring from a senior post in 1979. He died in 1995.

Air Chief Marshal Sir Christopher Foxley-Norris KCB DSO OBE

Christopher Foxley-Norris was born in Birkenhead in 1917, the son of a solicitor and was educated at Winchester College. He went up to Trinity College, Oxford where he read Greats (traditionally Roman and Greek history and philosophy). He was a member of the University Air Squadron and, in 1936, was commissioned in the Reserve of Air Force Officers. Two years later he relinquished this and received a commission in the RAFVR.

A career at the Bar had been planned, but, with the outbreak of war, Foxley-Norris was called up. He served in France with No 13 Squadron, flying Lysanders on Army Co-operation duties.

After his return to England Foxley-Norris volunteered for Fighter Command and went to No 5 OTU, Aston Down to convert to Hurricanes. Somebody was then apparently confused by Roman numerals and he was sent to No 111 Squadron at Drem, when he should have gone to No 3 Squadron at Turnhouse, where he arrived on 29 September 1940. He moved on to No 615 Squadron at Northolt in November.

On 26 February 1941 Foxley-Norris was shot down by Messerschmitt Bf 109s, but baled out safely.

He instructed in the UK and Canada, had a spell in Ferry Command and then went to No 143 Squadron in Coastal Command, as a flight commander, flying Beaufighters on anti-shipping strikes from North Coates in Lincolnshire and then St Eval, Cornwall. He was court martialled and acquitted over an alleged breach of security.

Foxley-Norris served in the Middle East, flying rocket-firing Beaufighters in seeking to deny supplies to German forces in the Aegean; he moved to command No 603 Squadron, also with Beaufighters. He returned to the UK and took command of No 143 Squadron, by now part of the Banff Mosquito Strike Wing, still though engaged in attacks on enemy shipping. On 25 September 1945 he was awarded the DSO.

His citation stated that:

'This officer has a long and distinguished record of operational flying. He has completed numerous sorties on his third tour of duty, during which he has operated against a wide range of enemy targets ... By his brilliant leadership, exceptional skill and determination, Wing Commander Foxley-Norris has contributed in good measure to the successes obtained.'

He would be described in his *Daily Telegraph* obituary as *'an exceptional low-level, ship-busting pilot and squadron commander during the Second World War.'*

Christopher Foxley-Norris's post war service included command of the Oxford University Air Squadron and of the RAF stations at Stradishall, Suffolk and West Malling, Kent. He was Assistant Chief of the Defence Staff (General) and led No 224 Group during the 'Indonesian Confrontation'. He was RAF Commander-in-Chief, Germany and from 1971 to his retirement in 1974 he was back in the UK as chief of personnel and logistics.

As well as the Chairmanship of the BBFA, Foxley-Norris spent six years as Chairman of the Cheshire Homes, founded by his friend from Oxford days, Leonard Cheshire VC.

Group Captain Thomas Percy Gleave CBE

After attendance at Westminster High School and Liverpool Collegiate School, Tom Gleave, who was born in 1908, worked for the Sefton Tanning Company. He was a founder member of the flying club at Hooton Park on the Wirral. He worked and flew for a time in Canada, then in 1930, joined the RAF on a short service commission. This became a permanent commission in 1936.

After completing his training, Tom Gleave went to No 1 Squadron, then equipped with the Armstrong Whitworth Siskin fighter. He attempted to become the first person to fly from the UK to Ceylon, but his effort and his Spartan aircraft came to a halt in a Turkish tree.

He served as an instructor and with the Oxford University Air Squadron, then became flying instructor with No 502 (Ulster) Special Reserve Squadron, taking the squadron into the Auxiliary Air Force and becoming adjutant and Chief Flying Instructor. He became bomber liaison officer in the Fighter Command operations room at Bentley Priory.

On 9 June 1940 Gleave took command of No 253, a Hurricane squadron then based at Kirton-in-Lindsey before a move to Turnhouse in Scotland.

He was posted to a ground job on 9 August and replaced as CO by Squadron Leader Harold Starr. However, Gleave persuaded his new boss that he was not required immediately and Starr agreed to him continuing with the squadron as a supernumerary. The squadron went to Prestwick and, on 29 August, south to Kenley.

The next day Tom Gleave claimed five Messerschmitt Bf 109s destroyed, but was credited with one destroyed and four probably destroyed. On the 31st Squadron Leader Starr baled out and was killed under his parachute by a German fighter. Command of the squadron reverted to Tom Gleave. However, later that day, over Biggin Hill, he was shot down and greviously burned.

Gleave would later recall how he had landed on farmland near the airfield, rolled up his parachute and walked until he came across a farm worker who took him to the house. There the pilot found himself in dispute with the lady of the house. She wanted him to get into bed until an ambulance arrived. Tom Gleave, knowing that he was in a frightful state, did not want to ruin her beautifully clean white sheets.

He was taken to Orpington Hospital and in due course arrived at the Queen Victoria Hospital, East Grinstead, where the work of the plastic surgery team there included building a new nose for him.

When The Guinea Pig Club was created at East Grinstead in 1941 Gleave was a founding committee member. In October that year he took command of RAF Manston. Four months later the Fairey Swordfish led by Lieutenant Commander Eugene Esmonde took off from Manston for their suicidal attack on the German naval force in what has gone down in history as the 'Channel Dash'. All the Swordfish were shot down and Esmonde was amongst those killed.

Gleave made the initial recommendation for the award of a posthumous Victoria Cross to Esmonde, the first time that a successful nomination for a member of the Royal Navy had come from an RAF officer.

Later in the war Gleave was a co-author of the overall air plan for Operation Overlord, the battle for Normandy.

Invalided out of the RAF in 1953, Gleave worked for the historical section of the Cabinet Office. He died in 1993.

Wing Commander Norman Patrick Watkins Hancock OBE DFC

Born in Streatham in 1919, Pat Hancock attended Croydon High School and Wimbledon Technical School. He joined the RAF on a short service commission and began his *ab initio* course in February 1939. He was posted to No 266 Squadron in November that year.

On 12 May 1940 Pilot Officer Hancock went to No 1 Squadron in France. Between 14 and 18 May he was attached to No 501 Squadron, but spent the posting moving around in lorries, a sign of the very fluid military situation at that time, rather than flying. Back with No 1 Squadron Hancock flew into action. In mid June he returned with the squadron to Northolt.

Pat Hancock fought through the Battle of Britain, then had spells with Nos 85 and 615 (County of Surrey) Squadrons before returning to No 1.

In April 1941 he sailed for Malta on HMS *Argus*. He transferred to HMS *Ark Royal*, then led seven Hurricanes off to Malta to join No 261 Squadron at RAF Hal Far. The squadron was disbanded in May and elements of it, including Hancock, were used in the re-forming of No 185 Squadron on 12 May. The next day Hancock became 'B' Flight commander when another Battle of Britain veteran, Flight Lieutenant Innes Westmacott, was wounded. Two months later Hancock earned a Mention in Despatches for an attack on launches carrying Italian frogmen seeking to raid Grand Harbour, Valletta.

His *Daily Telegraph* obituary would later say of this period of Hancock's life:

> 'Conditions on Malta were appalling. Hancock and his fellows were required to fight an air battle which was every bit as demanding as the Battle of Britain, surviving on a starvation diet which included fruit and nut chocolate full of maggots.
>
> 'This did not deter a ravenous Hancock, who reckoned if it was good enough for the maggots it was good enough for him. Cooking was near impossible, though efforts were made with oil which had been drained from crashed aircraft.'

Hancock went on to serve in Africa. He had a spell as an instructor at Gordon's Tree, Sudan. Later he was a Flight Commander and then CO of No 250 Squadron flying Kittyhawks. On 17 November 1942 Hancock, in difficult weather conditions, led an attack on Benina airfield, east of Benghazi, during which enemy aircraft in the air and on the ground were destroyed. He was awarded the DFC. He went on attachment with the Turkish and Egyptian air forces.

After the war Hancock commanded RAF Aberporth, was CO of No 11 Squadron, with Spitfires, in Japan and was a senior staff officer at HQ No 12 Group in the UK. He commanded No 33 Squadron, with de Havilland Hornets at Butterworth, Malaya. His final posting was as OC, RAF High Wycombe, the HQ of Bomber Command. After his retirement from the RAF in 1958 Pat Hancock ran a post office in Hampshire.

Group Captain John Hamar Hill CBE

Born in 1912, Johnnie Hill was educated at Dover College and took up a short service commission in the RAF in 1932. He served with No 19 Squadron and No 800 (Fleet Fighter) Squadron.

In September 1939 he was with No 85 Squadron for ops room duties.

He took command of No 87 Squadron in November that year in France, moving in February 1940 to command No 81 Squadron, also in France. The squadron had recently been re-formed and was undertaking communications duties using Tiger Moths.

With the Blitzkrieg well underway, Squadron Leader Hill returned to fighters on 16 May, assuming command of No 504 Squadron at Lille/Marcq airfield.

Three days later a remarkable series of adventures began for Hill when his Hurricane was shot down by a Messerschmitt Bf 109. He took to his parachute and was fired on by French civilians as he descended. He was arrested as fifth columnist by British soldiers, who then fired shots at him, which missed, because they thought he was reaching for a weapon. The soldiers then apparently stood by while Hill was attacked by French people. He was saved by a French officer who recognised him, but the soldiers apparently then tried to arrest him again.

Eventually Hill was placed on an ambulance train at Lille. However, between Le Touquet and Boulogne, Stukas dive-bombed the train and the driver and fireman abandoned their posts. Eventually Hill and another officer taught themselves to drive the locomotive and brought the train to Boulogne. Hill reached Dover from Dunkirk only to be arrested again as a fifth columnist.

Having recovered from that series of misfortunes Hill took command of No 222 Squadron at Kirton-in-Lindsey in early August 1940. At the end of the month this Spitfire squadron moved into the front line of the Battle of Britain at Hornchurch. He remained in the post until January 1941.

Between 1942 and 1945 Hill was on staff duties in New Zealand. In the late 1940s he was in Paris on the staff of the British Air Attaché. He retired from the RAF in 1960 and died in 1998.

Group Captain Sir Archibald Hope Bt OBE DFC

Archie Hope was born in 1912 and, in 1924, succeed his father as 17th Baronet of Craighall. Sir Archibald, as he had become, was educated at Eton College and Balliol College, Oxford, where he read Modern History. He was a member of the University Air Squadron.

Hope joined the Reserve of Air Force Officers in 1931 and later moved to the Auxiliary Air Force. He flew with No 601 (County of London) Squadron and was called to full time service, along with his colleagues, on 24 August 1939.

In Hope's time 601 had been allocated Harts, Demons and Gauntlets. Blenheims had arrived in early 1939 and they would be replaced by Hurricanes around a year later. Flying Officer Hope was the skipper of a Blenheim on the successful attack on the German seaplane base at Borkum on 28 November 1939.

In mid-May 1940 Hope was appointed 'A' Flight commander. He fought in France. His adventures there are recounted in *Men of the Battle of Britain*:

> 'On [18 May], *after sharing in the destruction of a Do 17, he was shot down by return fire and made a crash-landing in a field near Grevillers. On the 20th his aircraft was again damaged and he made another forced landing, this time at Merville.*
>
> 'On the 27th, *flying from Tangmere again, Hope was leading 601, when he was attacked by Bf 110s and shot down some five miles out from the coast between Calais and Dunkirk. He headed for land and flew as far east as possible, away from the advancing Germans.*
>
> '*Hope crash-landed on a beach, set fire to his Hurricane and was then taken by a French farmer to Bergues, where there was a British Brigade HQ. He was taken by lorry to the Dunkirk docks, spent a night on the dunes and went aboard the destroyer HMS* Wakeful *the next day. After landing at Dover, Hope phoned 601 and a Magister picked him up at Hawkinge. He was still carrying his parachute.*'

Archie Hope continued with the squadron in the Battle of Britain, achieving significant success and becoming CO on 19 August 1940. On 1 October the *London Gazette* announced his award of the DFC. His later postings during the war included commanding an Operational Training Unit, RAF Exeter and RAF Peterhead. He was made OBE in 1945.

Hope was a chartered accountant and a senior business figure after the war, sitting on the boards of a number of companies. He died in 1987.

Wing Commander William Pelham Hopkin DFC

Pelham Hopkin was born in 1921 and joined the RAF on a short service commission in 1939.

On 13 April 1940 he was posted to No 54 Squadron, flying Spitfires from Rochford. Shortly afterwards he went to No 6 OTU, Sutton Bridge. Having converted to Hurricanes, it was intended that he should go to a squadron in France. Instead, he returned to No 54 Squadron, although he then had a short spell at No 11 Group headquarters, Uxbridge.

Having returned to 54 Squadron, Pilot Officer Hopkin saw action with the squadron in the Battle of Britain, scoring a number of successes as the squadron moved between Rochford, Hornchurch and Catterick. On 12 September 1940 he was posted to No 602 Squadron at Westhampnett.

In early 1941 Hopkin was made a flight commander. His tour ended later in the year and he was awarded the DFC. He did not go back on operations. After the war he continued his RAF career in the Secretarial Branch and retired in 1967.

In the BBFA newsletter dated 26 July 1967, Air Commodore Donald MacDonell, as Chairman, wrote:

'If any member of your committee were to be singled out for commendation I think Pelham Hopkin ('Hoppy') deserves that distinction. For years now, he has served your committee with patience and enthusiasm and quite outstanding efficiency. His tact in covering up for my shortcomings as Chairman and his modesty and loyalty behind the scenes became part and parcel of our business. It is all the more sad that on retirement from the Service Hoppy has had to relinquish his office as Secretary. We owe him a big debt of gratitude.'

Air Commodore Aeneas Ranald Donald MacDonell CB DFC

MacDonell, usually known as 'Don' or 'Mac' in the RAF, was born in Russia in 1913. He would eventually become 22nd hereditary Chief of Clan MacDonell of Glengarry, a branch of Clan Donald. Glen Garry is north of Fort William in the Scottish Highlands. In correspondence in the BBFA files Major Sir Ralph Anstruther Bt, Equerry and Treasurer to Queen Elizabeth the Queen Mother follows Scottish tradition and begins letters, 'Dear Glengarry'.

After Hurstpierpoint School, MacDonell entered the RAF College Cranwell in 1932. He went on to serve with No 802 (Fleet Fighter) Squadron in Malta and then on board HMS *Glorious*. Time as an instructor and on a course at the Central Flying School followed. He then received a posting to the Air Ministry.

On 30 June 1940 MacDonell went to the Operational Training Unit at Aston Down, converted to Spitfires and joined No 64 Squadron at Kenley, as a supernumerary, on 19 July. He took command shortly afterwards.

During the Battle of Britain Squadron Leader MacDonell achieved a significant score. He was shot down by a Messerschmitt Bf 109 on 16 August, but baled out unhurt. His DFC was gazetted on 6 September.

In March 1941 MacDonell was shot down during a sweep over France and was taken prisoner. He was freed in April 1945 and later received a Mention in Despatches for distinguished services while in captivity. He retired from the RAF in 1964.

Group Captain Robert Wardlow Oxspring DFC (and two bars) AFC

Bobby Oxspring, the son of a Great War pilot, was born in Sheffield in 1919. After joining the RAF on a short service commission he began his training in March 1938. On 17 December that year he joined No 66 Squadron at Duxford at a point where the squadron was about to convert from Gloster Gauntlets to Supermarine Spitfires.

He joined No 263 Squadron, then tasked to take its Gladiators to Norway for the second time. However, Oxspring did not accompany 263 Squadron and returned to No 66, by now at Horsham St Faith, on 18 May 1940, after an absence of just over a week.

Oxspring achieved the status of an ace during the Battle of Britain and was made 'B' Flight commander on 5 September. On 25 October he was shot down in combat with Messerschmitt Bf 109s over Tunbridge Wells and baled out. He was slightly injured. In the spring of 1941 Oxspring was rested as an Operational Training Unit instructor.

He returned to operations later in the year, starting with a brief spell on No 616 Squadron, before going to No 41 Squadron as a Flight Commander. In January 1942 he assumed command of No 91 Squadron at Hawkinge. Six months later he became Officer Commanding No 72 Squadron at Biggin Hill. He was detached to command No 222 Squadron and took part in operations during the Dieppe raid by Canadian and British troops. He returned to No 72 and took the squadron to North Africa.

Oxspring later served with No 242 Group, co-ordinating Army requests for aerial assistance. He returned to the UK to a posting at Fighter Command HQ, Bentley Priory. In March 1944 he became Wing Leader No 24 Wing and, in June and July, was credited with destroying four V1s over London and Kent. He led No 141 Wing and then commanded the Detling Wing.

Later postings included at the Central Fighter Establishment, Tangmere, the United States Army Command and General Staff College, Fort Leavenworth, Kansas and at the Air Ministry in London.

Group Captain Oxspring retired from the RAF on 29 February 1968 and died in 1989.

Air Commodore Stanley Charles Widdows CB DFC

Charles Widdows was born in 1909. He joined the RAF in 1926, qualifying as a fitter and then, in September 1929 entered the RAF College, Cranwell as a Flight Cadet.

On graduating in 1931 he was posted to No 43 Squadron, moving on to No 29 Squadron in the following year. Widdows went on to serve in North Africa and Palestine, before becoming a test pilot at the Aeroplane and Armament Experimental Establishment at Martlesham Heath, Suffolk.

After a refresher course and conversion to Blenheims, Widdows took command of No 29 Squadron, which, in a night fighter role, operated Blenheims and, increasingly, from September 1940, Beaufighters, through the Battle of Britain and the Blitz of 1940/1941. Initially the squadron was based at Digby and Wellingore in Lincolnshire, moving, in March 1941, to West Malling, Kent.

Among the pilots who served under Widdows on 29 Squadron were 'Bob' Braham, one of the RAF's major night aces of the war and Guy Gibson, who had previously flown Hampdens in No 83 Squadron in Bomber Command and would return to that Command to lead No 106 Squadron and then form and command No 617 Squadron, earning a Victoria Cross for the attack on the German dams in May 1943.

Gibson would later recall that, immediately after arriving at No 29 Squadron, he observed with Widdows, in the Digby operations room, the development of Operation Moonlight Sonata, the devastating German attack on Coventry on the night of 14/15 November 1940.

Throughout his period in command of No 29 Squadron Charles Widdows flew assiduously at night seeking enemy aircraft. Eventually, on 13 March 1941, he was credited with destroying a Junkers Ju 88. In the following month he was awarded the DFC in recognition of his work with the squadron.

From June 1941 he commanded RAF West Malling and then held a range of staff jobs including with Nos 11 and 12 Groups and on General Eisenhower's staff.

Widdows remained in the RAF after the war and retired on 29 December 1958. He died in Guernsey, aged 100, in January 2010.

Air Vice-Marshal John Worrall CB DFC

John Worrall was born in 1911, educated at Cranleigh School and became a Flight Cadet at the RAF College, Cranwell in January 1930. He received a permanent commission at the end of 1931 and was posted to No 1 Squadron at Tangmere, equipped with the Armstrong Whitworth Siskin fighter.

For three years from 1933 Worrall served in Egypt with No 208 Squadron, operating in the Army Co-operation role, using aircraft that included the Hawker Audax. For much of Worrall's period with the squadron it was based at Heliopolis near Cairo. Later Worrall was in Peking as a languages student at the School of Oriental Studies.

In December 1939 John Worrall was posted to RAF Biggin Hill for ops duties. On 30 April 1940 he was posted to a Biggin Hill squadron, No 32, as a supernumerary. Six days later he took command of this Hurricane squadron.

'Baron' Worrall, as he was known, had a tough reputation, though he was apparently capable of humour to ease the tensions of the men he commanded. It was reported that on one occasion during the Battle of Britain No 32 Squadron was vectored on to an enemy formation the size of which, in the controller's estimation, kept growing. Eventually, Worrall retorted: '*No more information please, you are frightening me.*'

Off Dover, on 20 July, his Hurricane was hit and Worrall made a forced landing near Hawkinge. The aircraft burned out.

On 6 August he was awarded the DFC, the citation stating that:

'This officer's splendid leadership has been reflected in the work of his squadron, which has now destroyed forty-three enemy aircraft and possibly a further twenty-two. In July 1940 he led his squadron in a successful attack against a superior number of enemy aircraft, and assisted in destroying three of the enemy force. Squadron Leader Worrall has displayed great skill, courage and leadership.'

He was posted to the Biggin Hill control room on 16 August and one of the squadron's flight commanders, Mike 'Red Knight' Crossley, stepped up to replace him.

During the rest of the war, Worrall held various staff positions. He was at the RAF Staff College in 1945. He commanded RAF West Malling and, towards the end of his career, was Assistant Chief of the Air Staff (Training) and Senior Air Staff Officer, HQ Near East.

Retirement from the RAF occurred for John Worrall in 1963. He went into business, lived in Spain and died in 1988.

Wing Commander John Reginald Cass Young AFC

John Young was born in 1915. He was a cadet at Dartmouth Naval College, but left through illness. Later he qualified on HMS *Worcester* for direct entry into the Royal Navy but was not among the cadets taken on.

Young went to Canada, joined Canadian Pacific, learning to fly with the company at a time when it planned to launch air services. This intention was blocked for some years by the Canadian Government. Young returned to the UK and flew with the RAFO. He went up to St Catherine's College, Cambridge and worked during vacations as an assistant instructor at the Blackburn Flying School at Brough, Yorkshire.

Recalled to the active list in June 1939, Young went on an instructors' course at the Central Flying School, Upavon. He was then posted as flying instructor and Adjutant to No 41 Squadron at Catterick, but then spent several months in the same roles at No 603 (City of Edinburgh) Squadron, with a short detachment to No 609 (West Riding of Yorkshire) Squadron.

There was a considerable fondness for nicknames at 603 Squadron, among them 'Uncle George' Denholm, 'Stapme' Stapleton, 'Bolster' Boulter, 'Broody' Benson and 'Woolley Bear' Ritchie. John Young became 'Dobbin'. By his own account, this was a reference to the circumstance that, as an instructor, he was required to be rather more steady and, perhaps, plodding, than the lively weekend pilots around him.

'Dobbin' then moved from Spitfires to Hurricanes. He was with No 249 Squadron from May 1940, moving on, in quick succession, to Nos 306, 312 and 308 Squadrons. In 1941 he instructed at Nos 317 and 406 Squadrons. As a Squadron Leader he commanded No 289 Squadron at Kirknewton, West Lothian and opened the station. Officially the role of No 289 was anti-aircraft and searchlight liaison but John Young indicated in later life that pilots who had suffered from 'the shakes' in the French fighting and the Battle of Britain were attached to the squadron as part of the process of returning them to full operational capability. He was awarded the AFC.

Young later served at HQ Fighter Command, with No 264 Squadron flying Mosquitos in North Africa. He was OC Mediterranean Night Fighting Force, flying interdiction sorties over the Aegean.

After the war Young became a pilot with BOAC, rising to senior rank. He died in 2007.

Non Clasp holders

Malcolm Smith MBE

Malcolm Smith was born in Cleethorpes in 1935 and lived in north Lincolnshire for most of his life. He was called up for National Service, but decided to become a regular soldier, joining the Royal Electrical and Mechanical Engineers and serving in Hong Kong.

After leaving the Army Smith worked for de Havilland and it was in that period that his interest in aviation history began. His career path changed and he spent forty years with an importer of Danish bacon.

With his wife Joyce, Malcolm Smith was a regular visitor to the air show at Biggin Hill and to the nearby White Hart pub at Brasted, with its blackboard on which many veterans of the Battle of Britain had signed in chalk. Smith researched names on the board and began organizing Battle of Britain reunions at RAF Alconbury, a base for the United States Air Force in Cambridgeshire. This led to his appointment in 1995 as the first person, not holding the Battle of Britain Clasp, to serve as Secretary of the Battle of Britain Fighter Association.

He wrote articles for the *Grimsby Telegraph* on Battle of Britain airmen with local connections and a book, *Blitz on Grimsby*.

Smith retired from his post with the Fighter Association in 2006. He was awarded the MBE in the following year and died in 2010.

Group Captain Patrick Stuart Edwin Tootal OBE DL

Patrick Tootal was born in 1942. His father, Jack, served in the RAF in India, but volunteered for Bomber Command and was lost on the night of 24/25 February 1945.

Jack Tootal was the pilot of a Halifax of No 462 Squadron, RAAF. The squadron, based at Foulsham, Norfolk, was part of No 100 Group, tasked with disrupting German air defence systems. Flight Lieutenant Tootal's aircraft was shot down at Neuss in the Ruhr and the entire crew rest in the Rheinberg War Cemetery.

In his teens Patrick Tootal was a member of No 2291 (Ottershaw School) Squadron, Air Training Corps, rising to be the first Cadet Warrant Officer in Surrey.

In January 1960 he was accepted as a Flight Cadet at the RAF College, Cranwell. After graduation he became, in RAF terminology, a 'truck driver', flying Hastings and Hercules transport aircraft with Nos 24 and 36 Squadrons. He graduated from the RAF Staff College, Bracknell and then, at No 46 Group, served successively as Personal Staff Officer to two Battle of Britain veterans, Sir Denis Crowley-Milling and the future Lord Cameron.

After a tour as Air Intelligence Officer, Hong Kong, Tootal completed the Air Warfare Course and from 1977 to 1979 commanded No 70 (LXX) Squadron, operating the Hercules C.1 at Lyneham, Wiltshire. He commanded the RAF's contribution to providing humanitarian support for victims of the Kolwezi massacre in Zaire. He also led the evacuation of around 3,000 British and other nationals from Iran.

Tootal was on the battle planning staff during the Falklands War in 1982 and then planned the building of RAF Mount Pleasant on East Falkland. As a Group Captain he commanded RAF Hullavington in Wiltshire.

Later Tootal was Air Attaché in Madrid and Defence Attaché in Buenos Aires, the first person to hold that post after the resumption of diplomatic relations between the UK and Argentina. He retired from the RAF in 1993 and served as Kent County Field Officer of the Royal British Legion until 2005. He is the long serving Secretary of the Battle of Britain Memorial Trust.

One of Patrick Tootal's sons, Colonel Stuart Tootal, was awarded the DSO for his leadership of the 3rd Battalion, The Parachute Regiment in Afghanistan. Posthumous awards of the Victoria Cross and George Cross were made to men under his command.

Patrick Tootal's wife, Janet, was awarded the BEM in the 2014 New Year Honours for her work with the veterans of the battle through the BBFA and BBMT.

Air Chief Marshal Sir Hugh Caswall Tremenheere Dowding

Hugh Dowding was born at Moffat, Dumfreisshire in 1882 of Wiltshire ancestry. He attended St Ninian's Preparatory School in Moffat (where his father was headmaster) and went on to Winchester College. In 1899 he entered the Royal Military Academy at Woolwich, going on to be commissioned into Royal Garrison Artillery. He would serve in Gibraltar, Ceylon, Hong Kong and India.

Dowding's famous nickname, 'Stuffy' was given to him by fellow army officers and indicated a man, who on duty, was indeed stiff and humourless. However, according to the late Vincent Orange, one of Dowding's biographers, he was *'the soul of formal courtesy'* when dealing with subordinates and men and women who worked as hard as he did. He was a good listener and backed those who made a case. Early on in his career he acquired the reputation of being a maverick, which would stay with him.

Orange recorded that Dowding could be 'jovial' with polo or skiing companions and with his immediate family. In his book, *The Third Service*, Air Chief Marshal Sir Philip Joubert de la Ferte, wrote of Dowding, *'Out of office hours he could be an extremely entertaining companion, having a fund of good stories and a quick wit with which to tell them.'*

A WAAF who was stationed at Bentley Priory during the Second World War recalled an occasion when she was leaving the apparently deserted building late at night. She heard a noise behind her and found that Air Chief Marshal Dowding had appeared. He looked exhausted, but touched his cap and opened the door for her.

Dowding was accepted at the Staff College, Camberley in 1912. In the following year he was promoted to captain and qualified as a pilot, having paid for his own tuition. Dowding joined the Royal Flying Corps on the outbreak of war in 1914, later going to the Western Front, initially as an observer with No 6 Squadron. He reverted to pilot status and then became a staff officer, before returning to England and the command of an experimental wireless unit at Brooklands in Surrey. Later in the war he commanded No 16 Squadron and No 9 Wing, both in France.

Dowding received a permanent commission as a Group Captain and commanded No 1 Group at Kenley, before staff appointments, including service in Iraq. He was Director of Training at the Air Ministry. He went back to the Middle East and wrote reports on the security situation there which impressed his superiors. Air Vice-Marshal Dowding joined the Air Council in 1930 as Air Member for Supply and Research. In 1933 he became an Air Marshal and was made KCB. From 1935 his title was Air Member for Research and Development.

In July 1936 Dowding was appointed to lead the newly created Fighter Command, one of a number of Commands established at that time. According to Air Marshal Sir Peter Wykeham, Dowding, wearing civvies, arrived at Bentley Priory for the first time in his new role, on 14 July. The place was only staffed by a holding party and the most senior person available to show the new Commander-in-Chief around was Sergeant Cornthwaite. His new boss was not displeased by such lack of ceremony.

> '*Together*,' wrote Wykeham, '*they explored the Priory and grounds. Inland Area may have led an unexciting life, but they had certainly not neglected the magnificent surroundings entrusted to them. The great house still preserved the air of a nobleman's mansion, the lawns were shaved and the shrubs and hedges clipped. To the east of the house, a fine sports field was set against a background of splendid cedars. Mr Hall, the gardener for many years, still served the Air Ministry as he had served the former owners.*'

Early in 1937 Dowding was promoted to Air Chief Marshal. Under his command the defensive system initiated in the First World War and developed since that time, grew to the point where it was able to play a decisive part in the fighting of 1940 as 'the Dowding system'.

In 1939 Dowding's period at Fighter Command was scheduled to come to an end and it was planned that his replacement would be Air Marshal Sir Christopher Courtney. Partly through the fact that Courtney was injured in an air crash, this change did not take place. Various extensions to Dowding's tenure at Bentley Priory were decided upon. Thus Dowding was still in office to prepare Fighter Command for and fight what came to be called the Battle of Britain. The period in the lead up to the battle included the efforts to avoid more and more Hurricane fighters being sent to be lost in the Battle of France.

Perhaps the manner of Dowding's removal from Fighter Command, as we now know, almost in the hour of his triumph, and the failure to find a further suitable role for him, are more perplexing than the fact that he left Bentley Priory.

There was intrigue against him, both at the Air Ministry and amongst some of his subordinates. At the same time there were views sincerely held by some senior officers and politicans that there were reasons to make a change. Dowding's age, the strain he had been under and the need to adapt to fighting a new air war at night, with the onset of the Blitz, were factors in some minds. A factor too was his apparent unwillingness to ensure that the Commanders-in-Chief of Fighter Command's Nos 11 and 12 Groups were working together and obeying his orders.

Nonetheless, as we can now see it, the architects of triumph at one of the turning points of British history, Keith Park at No 11 Group, as well as Dowding, were removed in a most churlish manner. Park eventually returned to front line command and proved his brilliance again, though it might be argued that his career never fully recovered from his treatment in 1940.

Dowding was told that he would go by Sinclair, Secretary of State for Air, in a meeting on 13 November 1940 and left Fighter Command on 25 November.

Now came the failure to find suitable war work for such an exceptional leader. Dowding led an aircraft-purchasing mission to the United States and subsequently headed a project to seek ways of achieving economies in the RAF. He was hardly suited to the roles and officially retired on 14 July 1942.

Honours did come to Dowding. Before the battle had ended he had been made GCB. In June 1943 he became Lord Dowding of Bentley Priory. Efforts to gain him promotion to Marshal of the Royal Air Force were fruitless, despite an intervention by the King. When Dowding died in 1970 his ashes were buried in the RAF Chapel in Westminster Abbey. In 1988, HM Queen Elizabeth the Queen Mother unveiled a statue of Dowding outside the RAF Church of St Clement Danes in The Strand in Central London.

Dowding is memorialized in Moffat where he was born. The former St Ninian's School, closed in the 1980s and for a time in danger of becoming derelict, is now a home in the care of the Royal Air Forces Association, named Dowding House. In the town's Station Park there is an impressive memorial in sandstone and bronze. Another memorial to Lord Dowding is situated in Calverley Park, Tunbridge Wells, the town where he died.

"'Stuffy" Dowding was a great commander and to this day we, his pilots, remember him with respect and affection and think he should have been made an MRAF' – Wing Commander John Beazley writing in 2003.

'*The only commander who won one of the few decisive battles in history and got sacked for his pains'* – Marshal of the Royal Air Force Sir Arthur Harris.

'*One of those great men whom this country miraculously produces in times of peril'* – Denis Healey, Secretary of State for Defence, speaking at the interment of Lord Dowding's ashes in Westminster Abbey.

Air Chief Marshal Sir Keith Park

Keith Park was born in Thames, in the North Island of New Zealand in 1892. He served with the New Zealand artillery at Gallipoli, moved to the Royal Artillery and then the Royal Flying Corps. From 1917 he flew Bristol Fighters with No 48 Squadron in France, commanding the squadron from 10 April 1918. He was awarded the MC and bar and DFC.

Between the wars he held a varied series of appointments typical of a rising RAF officer including service at HQ Air Defence of Great Britain, command of No 111 Squadron and of RAF Northolt.

As a Group Captain he was Air ADC to the King from January 1937 and became Officer Commanding RAF Tangmere in December that year. In July 1938 Air Commodore Park became Senior Air Staff Officer at Fighter Command. Promoted to the rank of Air Vice-Marshal, he was appointed Air Officer Commanding No 11 Group, placing him at the forefront of decision making during the Battle of Britain. He was moved to an Air Training post in December 1940, leading many to claim that his contribution to winning the battle was not appreciated. He returned to operational duty, serving in the Middle East and Malta and as Air Commander-in-Chief, South East Asia Command.

Park was retired from the RAF in 1946, a decision that he had not expected and which deeply shocked him. Much of his later life was spent in New Zealand. He held posts in aviation and supported charities. He died in 1975.

Park has been described as tougher than Dowding when it came to removing those who failed to perform. He had few close friends and did not enjoy socialising outside his family. He could appear aloof, yet could also display great charm.

'If ever any one man won the Battle of Britain (Park) did. I don't believe it is realised how much that one man, with his leadership, his calm judgement and his skill did to save not only this country but the world.' – MRAF Lord Tedder, CAS, speaking at the annual dinner of the New Zealand Society in London, February 1947.

'What Park achieved in the Battle of Britain is in itself enough to place him amongst the great commanders of history. But his performance in 1940 was not a one-off. In 1942 in Malta Park took the offensive and turned Kesselring's defeat into a rout. After that he directed the air operations that enabled Slim to expel the Japanese from Burma. He was as adept at offence as he was at defence and, like Wellington, he never lost a battle. His record makes him today, without rival, the greatest fighter commander in the history of air warfare.' – Stephen Bungay, *The Most Dangerous Enemy.*

'The awesome responsibility for this country's survival rested squarely on Keith Park's shoulders. Had he failed, "Stuffy" Dowding's foresight, determination and achievement would have counted for nought.' Group Captain Douglas Bader addressing the memorial service for Park on 12 September 1975, at St Clement Danes Church.

Marshal of the Royal Air Force Sir Dermot Boyle

Boyle was born in 1904 at Rathdowney in what is now County Laois in the Republic of Ireland. He attended St Columba's College, Dublin and became a cadet at Cranwell in 1922. He would retain an affection for Cranwell and an interest in its affairs for the rest of his life.

Having graduated Boyle served with No 17 Squadron at Hawkinge, where he flew the Sopwith Snipe fighter. He was posted to Iraq, then had excellent opportunities to demonstrate his skill as a pilot, serving as an instructor and taking part in Hendon air displays. He served with the Auxiliary Air Force, including as Assistant Adjutant and Qualified Flying Instructor with No 601 (County of London) Squadron, and in a staff post in India. For more than two years he was Chief Flying Instructor at Cranwell.

After the outbreak of the Second World War Boyle was in France with the Advanced Air Striking Force as a staff officer. He served at Bomber Command HQ and, from November 1940, had the second spell of his career commanding No 83 Squadron in Bomber Command, by now equipped with

Hampdens. From February 1941 Group Captain Boyle spent almost a year as Assistant Secretary of the Committee of Imperial Defence, a post more wide-ranging than it sounds and right at the centre of affairs.

Boyle was then appointed OC RAF Stradishall and went on to be Senior Air Staff Officer, No 83 Group.

Post war appointments included a spell as Assistant Commandant, RAF Staff College. From April 1953 he was Air Officer Commanding-in-Chief at Fighter Command. In 1956 he became Chief of the Air Staff, despite never having been a member of the Air Council. On the other hand he was the first former Cranwell cadet to lead the RAF. His tenure lasted until the end of 1959 and he was therefore embroiled in the Suez crisis and the battle in that era against major cuts in the RAF. He died in 1993.

The historian Air Commodore Henry Probert wrote of Boyle:

'He was one of the great father figures of the RAF. Superb flying ability, great staff skills, inspiring leadership, dominating presence, power to command an audience, charm, kindliness: such qualities made him one of the most respected and best-loved of all the RAF's high commanders.'

Marshal of the Royal Air Force Sir Thomas Pike

Thomas Pike was born in Lewisham, south east London in 1906 and educated at Bedford School. He entered the RAF College, Cranwell in 1924. He later served with No 56 Squadron at Biggin Hill, flying first the Gloster Grebe and then the Siskin. He was an instructor at the Central Flying School, where he was a member of the aerobatic team, before service in the Middle East.

In 1938 and early 1939, as a Squadron Leader, Pike was Chief Flying Instructor at No 10 Flying Training School, Ternhill, Shropshire. Time at the Air Ministry followed before, in February 1941, he was appointed Officer Commanding, No 219 Squadron, as a Wing Commander. Leading the squadron from Tangmere, he flew Beaufighters at night, being awarded the DFC and bar.

Further postings took him to the staff of No 11 Group and the command of RAF North Weald. He went to the Middle East again and from early 1944 was Senior Air Staff Officer at HQ Desert Air Force.

After the war Thomas Pike attended the Imperial Defence College and commanded No 11 Group. He served with NATO, returned to the UK to become Assistant and the Deputy Chief of the Air Staff. He became Air

Officer, Commanding in Chief Fighter Command and, from 1 January 1960, Chief of the Air Staff, remaining in post for four years.

Most unusually the post of CAS proved not to be the end of Sir Thomas Pike's active career because he became Deputy Supreme Commander Allied Powers Europe, under the leadership of the American General Lyman Lemnitzer. This appointment lasted until March 1967. He was later President of the Royal Air Forces Association and died in 1983.

Citation for the award of the Bar to the Distinguished Flying Cross – *London Gazette* 30 May 1941:

> '*Wing Commander Thomas Geoffrey PIKE DFC (16202), No 219 Squadron.*
>
> '*This officer has displayed outstanding skill and keenness in his efforts to seek and destroy the enemy at night. One night recently while his aerodrome was being bombed, he took off to engage the attackers when the aerodrome was illuminated by the glare from a large number of incendiary bombs.*'

People who have played an important role in Battle of Britain commemoration

Daisy Alcock (1903–1996)

Daisy Alcock was born in Wednesfield, Staffordshire and grew up there in the 18th century house at New Cross Farm, where she would also live for much of her adult life. Her father, Ralph Alcock, ran the farm and was in addition a master carpenter. Daisy attended Wolverhampton Girls' Grammar School. Described as 'diminutive' as an adult, she lectured and undertook calligraphy commissions from a studio in Kensington. She was buried with her parents in Holy Trinity churchyard, Heath Town, not far from her home.

After her death the farmhouse deteriorated, partly as a result of arson attacks and was eventually demolished.

Paul Fulcrand Delacour de Labilliere (1879–1946)

Paul de Labilliere was the son of Francis de Labilliere, a barrister, and his wife Adelaide. He was educated at Harrow School and Oxford, being ordained in 1902. He became a curate in Liverpool and Plymouth before being appointed chaplain to the Bishop of Durham. For a time his ministry took him to South Africa, where he married Ester Morkel. They had a son and daughter.

While de Labilliere was a temporary chaplain to the Forces from 1916 to 1919 he served in Egypt and was Mentioned in Despatches. Later he was Rector of Methley, near Leeds, Suffragan Bishop of Knaresborough and Archdeacon of Leeds. In 1938 he became Dean of Westminster, the announcement of the appointment having been made in November 1937.

The Westminster Abbey website records:

> 'During his time at the Abbey he did much to enhance the services and during the war showed many hundreds of visiting troops around the Abbey. His home, the Deanery, was blitzed in 1941 and the King and Queen offered him accommodation at Buckingham Palace but he preferred to stay within the Abbey precincts. A contemporary described him as tall, slender with white hair, who dressed beautifully and was punctual.'

Dean de Labilliere died of a brain haemorrhage on 28 April 1946. His wife died on 18 March 1954. The ashes of both are buried in the nave of the Abbey.

Hugh Ray Easton (1906–1965)
The son of a doctor, Hugh Easton was educated at Wellington College and the University of Tours. He studied the craft of stained glass and established a studio in Cambridge. He served as an officer in the Royal Naval Volunteer Reserve in the Second World War and undertook a censorship role in the Ministry of Information.

After the war Easton returned to the design of stained glass, basing himself in London. He died of cancer aged 58.

Sir Bruce Stirling Ingram (1877–1963)
Bruce Ingram was born in London. His father, William James Ingram, was managing director of the *Illustrated London News*, '*The world's first illustrated weekly newspaper*'. He was created a baronet, and, as a Liberal, was representing Boston, Lincolnshire in the House of Commons at the time of Bruce's birth. The father of William James had founded the *Illustrated London News*. Bruce's middle name, as was common at the time and for many years afterwards, was the maiden name of his mother, Mary Eliza Collingwood Stirling.

The young Bruce was educated at Winchester College and went up to Trinity College, Oxford, where he graduated with a third class honours degree in jurisprudence. He gained some experience with a printing company, but then joined his family's business. Aged 22, in 1900, he was appointed editor of the *Illustrated London News*. He would retain this post until his death sixty-three years later, taking the magazine, with considerable modernisation along the way, from the days of the Boer War to the period of the Cuban missile crisis. He also held the post of chairman of the company for many years and was editor of *The Sketch*.

The *Oxford Dictionary of National Biography* says that:

> '*Ingram was always an active editor, and those who worked with him recall that even in his eighties he would crawl around the floor of his editorial office laying out the photographs for each weekly issue. He was astute in his judgement of writers—he chose G.K. Chesterton in 1905 to write the weekly Notebook feature, and on Chesterton's death in 1936 picked the young Arthur Bryant to succeed him. Inevitably some parts of the paper reflected some of his prejudices: he was suspicious of modern art, so Picasso was ignored; and he was tone-deaf, so music tended to be neglected. But such eccentricities did not tarnish his reputation as an editor, which rested securely on his achievements in communicating ... the actuality and atmosphere of Britain, its character, temper, and achievements, in a style that was not equalled.*'

Before the First World War Ingram became an officer in the East Kent Yeomanry. In 1916 he transferred to the Royal Garrison Artillery. He served in France, reached the rank of captain (he would often be referred to as 'Captain Ingram' in later life) and was awarded the MC and made OBE (Military). Despite this active service, Ingram managed to maintain much control over his key publication, which was seen by the Government as a valuable means of making its position known abroad.

The same proved true in the Second World War when Ingram remained at his publishing post on a daily basis, ignoring the Blitz, although bombing destroyed much of the company archive.

From his youth Ingram was keenly interested in archaeology. He became an avid collector of art, especially nautical subjects and a great benefactor to the National Maritime Museum. He was highly regarded in the art world and had a reputation for considerable generosity in loaning works from his vast collection for public display.

Ingram's home at Great Pednor Manor, Buckinghamshire, at the hamlet of Pednor in the Chiltern Hills, contained domestic wall paintings, some of which were discovered in December 1939, during Ingram's residence, when alterations to the house were being carried out. Bruce Ingram was knighted in 1950.

Sir Albert Edward Richardson (1880–1964)

Richardson was born in Hackney, the son of a printer. On leaving school he worked in the offices of various architects. He established a partnership with Charles Lovett Gill and designed the facade of London's Regent Street Polytechnic. He also worked on the New Theatre, now the Opera House, in Manchester and was the author/co-author of books on architecture

For two years in the Great War, Richardson was an officer in the Royal Flying Corps. He served at the School of Military Aeronautics at Reading. For many years from 1919 he was Professor of Architecture and then Professor Emeritus at the Bartlett School of Architecture, University College, London. According to the *Oxford Dictionary of National Biography*:

> '*Not by temperament an academic, nor indeed a scholar of the more disciplined kind, his history lectures were rhetorical improvisations, made wonderfully vivid by a rare talent for impromptu graphic demonstration.*'

At the close of the Second World War, Richardson formed a partnership with his son in law, E.A.S. Houfe. Their work included restoration of buildings damaged by enemy action, including St James's Church, Piccadilly, London and, also in the capital, Trinity House, Tower Hill.

In the 1950s Richardson was President of the Royal Academy. He was a member of the Royal Fine Arts Commission and was appointed KCVO in 1956.

Sir Ronald Deane Ross Bt MC KC (1888–1958)

Ronald Ross was the son of Sir John Ross, last Lord Chancellor of Ireland. Ronald was educated at Eton College and at Trinity College, Cambridge. He was called to the Bar in 1913. He was already serving with the North Irish Horse when the First World War broke out and served in France, including the retreat from Mons in 1914.

In 1929 he went to the House of Commons, returned unopposed as Ulster Unionist MP for Londonderry. He continued as an MP until 1951 and for a time was Chairman of the Ulster Unionist MPs at Westminster. On his father's death in 1935 he became the second Baronet.

From 1941 he served in the Royal Armoured Corps, was a British delegate to the Council of Europe in Strasbourg and, from 1957, represented the Government of Northern Ireland in London.

Viscount Thurso (formerly Sir Archibald Henry Macdonald Sinclair Bt) (1890–1970)

Archie Sinclair's father was an officer in the Scots Guards. Archie was quickly orphaned, his mother, daughter of a New York businessman, dying a few weeks after her son's birth and his father five years later.

Various relatives looked after the boy. '*He had no real home but rather a series of houses where he would stay until his presence became burdensome,*' wrote his biographer, Gerard De Groot. Sinclair attended Eton College and then was a cadet at Sandhurst.

De Groot went on to note that, '*Despite the disadvantages of his youth, Archie Sinclair became a confident, gregarious young man, adored and in turn enchanted by Edwardian high society.*'

He certainly created a favourable impression on the then Prime Minister, H.H. Asquith, who, having met Sinclair at dinner just before the First World War, recorded that he was:

> '*one of the "nicest" young men I have met for a long time … he is only 23, owns 100,000 acres or thereabouts, is in the 2nd Life Guards, and when in London flies every morning before breakfast. In addition he has good looks and manners, a slight but attractive stammer and wears a kilt of a sober but striking pattern.*'

By this time he was Sir Archibald, having succeeded to the family Baronetcy in 1912 on the death of his grandfather.

The dinner at which the meeting with Asquith took place was hosted by Winston Churchill, then First Lord of the Admiralty. Churchill and Sinclair spent much of their lives as close friends, although the relationship was sometimes complicated.

Flying and polo were among their common interests. The present Viscount Thurso recalls, as a child, playing with a ball outdoors in the presence of his grandfather. The old man used a T-shaped walking stick. When the ball came towards him he would quickly reverse the stick and thump it back to his grandson, polo fashion.

When Churchill commanded a battalion of the Royal Scots Fusiliers on the Western Front in the Great War Sinclair was his second-in-command.

Sinclair acted as an aide to Churchill after the war, in the Government offices held by the latter. Sinclair entered the House of Commons in 1922 as a Liberal, representing Caithness and Sutherland. He played an active part in the complicated politics of the twenties and thirties and served as Secretary of State for Scotland. From 1935 he was Chairman of the Parliamentary Liberal Party. He and Churchill worked together against the Munich agreement.

On the outbreak of war Sinclair refused to accept office under Neville Chamberlain. He was one of those who attacked Chamberlain in the 'Norway debate' in early May 1940 and, after Churchill had become Prime Minister on 10 May, Sinclair was appointed Secretary of State for Air.

It has been suggested frequently that Sinclair was treated without respect, even bullied, by Churchill during the war. It can be argued that almost all senior figures had been dealt with in that way by Churchill at some point. Sinclair seems to have absorbed the Prime Minister's sometimes hectoring manner without undue concern. He also survived the machinations and hostility of Lord Beaverbrook, during the press baron's time as Minister of Aircraft Production.

One man who would change his view of Sinclair's relationship with Churchill was 'Jock' Colville, a private secretary to Chamberlain, Churchill and Attlee. Colville's diaries gave the impression of the Secretary of State for Air as under the Prime Ministerial thumb, but in the 1980s Sir John Colville would say that he no longer took the same view.

Within months of his appointment to the Air Ministry Sinclair was embroiled in the controversy surrounding the departure of Sir Hugh Dowding from Fighter Command. Despite claims to the contrary, Sinclair did see Dowding face to face at the climax of the matter – on 13 November 1940.

From time to time during the war there were offers made to Sinclair – for example, to become Viceroy of India – which would have taken him away from the Air Ministry. He determinedly remained in post until the break up of the coalition government in May 1945.

Sinclair lost his Parliamentary seat in the General Election of 1945 and failed to regain it. He was Lord Lieutenant of Caithness from 1919 to 1964. His later years were blighted by ill health.

Appendix I

The 1943 Casualty List

The list of Fighter Command airmen for the Westminster Abbey Roll of Honour as submitted by Air Marshal Sir Trafford Leigh-Mallory, Air Officer Commanding in Chief, Fighter Command, January 1943. No attempt has been made to correct any errors in this document as it was produced.

Battle of Britain

Detailed below are those members of the flying forces of the Fighter Command who lost their lives as a result of the fighting during the Battle of Britain – 8 August – 31 October 1940.

Royal Air Force
Pilots
Pilot Officer Hugh Charles Adams
Pilot Officer Raymond Andre Charles Aeberhardt
Pilot Officer Harold John Akroyd
Sergeant Harold Henry Allgood
Sergeant Leslie Charles Allton
Pilot Officer Christopher John Drake Andreae
Sergeant Stanley Andrew
Pilot Officer Dennis Garth Ashton
Pilot Officer Harold Derrick Atkinson DFC
Pilot Officer Ronald Atkinson
Sergeant David Hart Ayers
Sergeant Charles Albert Henry Ayling
Squadron Leader John Vincent Clarence Badger
Pilot Officer John Cyril Lindsay Dyson Bailey
Sergeant Eric Debnam Baker
Sergeant Harold David Baker

Sergeant Eric Samuel Bann
Sergeant John Keell Barker
Flying Officer Nathanial John Merriman Barry
Sergeant Sidney Baxter
Sergeant Edward Alan Bayley
Pilot Officer Walter Beaumont
Pilot Officer Robert Wilfred Garth Beley
Flying Officer John Swift Bell
Pilot Officer Noel John Victor Benson
Pilot Officer John Benzie
Flight Lieutenant Hugh Richard Aden Beresford
Flight Sergeant Frederick George Berry DFM
Sergeant Herbert Ernest Black
Pilot Officer John Wellburn Bland
Sergeant Henry Albert Bolton
Pilot Officer Camille Robespierre Bonseigneur
Sergeant Glendon Bulmar Booth
Flying Officer John Eric Boulton
Flight Lieutenant Charles Earle Bowen
Pilot Officer Nigel Greenstreet Bowen
Flying Officer John Greer Boyle
Flying Officer Guy Rawstron Branch EGM
Sergeant John Joseph Brimble
Pilot Officer John William Broadhurst
Pilot Officer Dennis Owen Matthew Browne
Acting Flight Lieutenant David Campbell Bruce
Sergeant Norman Brumby
Pilot Officer John Bryson
Sergeant Samuel Leslie Butterfield DFM
Pilot Officer Eric Burgoyne
Flying Officer Percival Ross-Frames Burton
Pilot Officer Francis Walter Cale
Acting Flight Lieutenant William Percival Cambridge
Pilot Officer Norman Neil Campbell
Pilot Officer Philip Melville Cardell
Pilot Officer Charles Frederick Cardnell
Flying Officer Peter Edward George Carter

Pilot Officer Herbert Robert Case
Flying Officer Frederick Norman Cawse
Pilot Officer Harry Hutchinson Chalder
Pilot Officer Allison George Chomley
Sergeant John McBean Christie
Pilot Officer Arthur William Clarke
Pilot Officer John Kenneth Grahame Clifton
Pilot Officer Donald Gordon Cobden
Acting Flight Lieutenant John Hunter Coghlan DFC
Flying Officer Peter Collard DFC
Sergeant George Richard Collett
Pilot Officer Peter Woodruff Comely
Flight Lieutenant Stanley Dudley Pierce Connors DFC
Pilot Officer Jack Harry Hamilton Copeman
Pilot Officer George Henry Corbett
Flying Officer William Hugh Coverley
Pilot Officer Kenneth Henry Cox
Flying Officer Peter Guerin Crofts
Pilot Officer John Dallas Crossman
Pilot Officer John Cruttenden
Flight Lieutenant John Laurence Gilchrist Cunningham
Flying Officer John Wintringham Cutts
Flying Officer Brian William Jesse D'Arcy-Irvine
Pilot Officer John Arthur Joseph Davey
Pilot Officer Alfred Eric Davies
Flying Officer Paul John Davies-Cooke
Flight Lieutenant Carl Raymond Davis DFC
Flying Officer Richard Stephen Demetriadi
Wing Commander John Scatliff Dewar DSO DFC
Flying Officer Robert Basil Dewey
Pilot Officer William Gordon Dickie
Sergeant John Holt Dickinson
Flying Officer Ivor Benison Difford
Flying Officer Michael Duke Doulton
Pilot Officer George James Drake
Flying Officer John Fraser Drummond DFC
Sergeant Leslie Arthur Dyke

Sergeant William Lawrence Dymond DFM
Pilot Officer Hilary Patrick Michael Edridge
Pilot Officer Harry Davies Edwards
Sergeant Gerald Henry Edworthy
Sergeant Edward James Egan
Sergeant Douglas William Elcome
Sergeant John Hugh Mortimer Ellis
Pilot Officer Charles Edward English
Sergeant Peter Raoul Eyles
Sergeant John Robinson Farrow
Sergeant Alan Norman Feary
Sergeant Stanley Allen Fennemore
Acting Flight Lieutenant Henry Michael Ferriss DFC
Flying Officer Basil Mark Fisher
Pilot Officer William Mead Lindsley Fiske
Pilot Officer Robert David Spittal Fleming
Pilot Officer George Mathwin Forrester
Pilot Officer Colin Dunstone Francis
Sergeant Robert Henry Braund Fraser
Sergeant Eric Thomas George Frith
Sergeant Leonard Arthur Garvey
Pilot Officer Geoffrey Norman Gaunt
Flying Officer James Gillan
Flight Lieutenant Kenneth McLeod Gillies
Pilot Officer Keith Reginald Gillman
Sergeant Alexander George Girdwood
Sergeant Geoffrey Gledhill
Flying Officer Richard Lindsay Glyde DFC
Flying Officer Claude Waller Goldsmith
Flying Officer Harold Ingham Goodall
Sergeant Charles Goodwin
Flying Officer Henry Macdonald Goodwin
Pilot Officer William Hugh Gibson Gordon
Flight Lieutenant William Ernest Gore DFC
Sergeant Malcolm Gray
Pilot Officer Felix Stafford Gregory
Flying Officer Dennis Neve Grice

Pilot Officer Peter Stackhouse Gunning
Pilot Officer Edward Maurice Gunter
Pilot Officer John Pinter Gurteen
Sergeant Leonard Northwood Guy
Sergeant Cyril Haigh
Flight Lieutenant Noel Mudie Hall AFC
Sergeant Derrick Wilson Halton
Flight Lieutenant Harry Raymond Hamilton
Flying Officer David Harry Wellsted Hanson
Flying Officer John Reginald Hardacre
Pilot Officer Frederic Norman Hargreaves
Pilot Officer David Stewart Harrison
Pilot Officer John Howard Harrison Harrold
Sergeant Redvers Percival Hawkings
Sergeant Frederick Bernard Hawley
Sergeant Denis Arnold Helcke
Pilot Officer Norman Bagshaw Heywood
Sergeant William Burley Higgins
Pilot Officer Cecil Henry Hight
Pilot Officer Howard Perry Hill Bryan Lillie Hillcoat
Pilot Officer Colin Anthony Hobson
Pilot Officer Douglas William Hogg
Pilot Officer Richard Malzard Hogg
Pilot Officer Dennis Frederick Holland
Sergeant Kenneth Christopher Holland
Squadron Leader Hilary Richard Lionel Hood
Flying Officer Ralph Hope
Sergeant Oliver Vincent Houghton
Pilot Officer Peter Howes
Flight Lieutenant David Price Hughes
Acting Flight Lieutenant Paterson Clarence Hughes DFC
Acting Squadron Leader Caesar Barrand Hull DFC
Squadron Leader Philip Algernon Hunter DSO
Pilot Officer Richard Ralph Hutley
Flight Lieutenant Maurice Milne Irving
Flying Officer Michael Jebb
Acting Flight Lieutenant Robert Voase Jeff

Sergeant George William Jefferys
Pilot Officer David Nicholas Owen Jenkins
Sergeant Joseph Inkerman Johnson
Pilot Officer James Thomas Johnston
Pilot Officer John Sinclair Bucknall Jones
Pilot Officer Joseph Trever Jones
Pilot Officer Peter Frank Kennard-Davis
Pilot Officer Peter Lewis Kenner
Sergeant Michael Keymer
Squadron Leader Eric Bruce King
Pilot Officer Martyn Aurel King
Flying Officer Peter James Christopher King
Sergeant David Ian Kirton
Flying Officer Hugh Michael Stanford Lambert
Pilot Officer Gerald Archibald Langley
Sergeant John Lansdell
Pilot Officer Joseph Emile Paul Laricheliere
Pilot Officer John Gage Lecky
Flying Officer Richard Hugh Antony Lee DSO DFC
Pilot Officer John Desmond Lenahan
Sergeant Ronald Little
Sergeant Philip David Lloyd
Squadron Leader Terence Gunion Lovell-Gregg
Acting Flight Lieutenant Reginald Eric Lovett DFC
Flying Officer Derek Charles MacCaw
Pilot Officer Donald Kennedy MacDonald
Sergeant Peter Roy Charles McIntosh
Pilot Officer John Woffenden McKenzie
Sergeant Alexander McNay
Pilot Officer Gerald Hamilton Maffett
Pilot Officer Ernest Edward Males
Pilot Officer Kenneth Manger DFC
Sergeant Edward Marton
Pilot Officer Roy Achille Marchand
Sergeant Henry James Marsh
Pilot Officer John Romney Mather
Flying Officer Henry Key Fielding Matthews

Pilot Officer James Reginald Bryan Meaker DFC
Flying Officer Miles John Miley
Pilot Officer Rogers Freeman Garland Miller
Pilot Officer William Henry Millington DFC
Flying Officer Lancelot Robert George Mitchell
Flying Officer George Edward Moberly
Pilot Officer Cecil Robert Montgomery
Sergeant Herbert Francis Montgomery
Pilot Officer Henry Wollaston Moody
Sergeant Joseph Pearson Morrison
Acting Flight Lieutenant Ian James Muirhead DFC
Sergeant William John Neville
Sergeant Dennis Noble
Sergeant Philip Purchall Norris
Squadron Leader Joseph Somerton O'Brien DFC
Pilot Officer Johannes Roelof Stephanus Oelofse
Sergeant Trevor Guest Oldfield
Flying Officer Derek Keppel Coleridge O'Malley
Flying Officer Desmond Hugh O'Neill
Pilot Officer Eric Orgias
Sergeant Kenneth Bruce Parker
Acting Flight Lieutenant Denis Geach Parnall
Pilot Officer Stuart Boyd Parnall
Acting Flight Lieutenant James Alfred Paterson
Flying Officer Aberconway John Sefton Pattinson
Sergeant Kenneth Clifton Pattison
Pilot Officer William Blair Pattullo
Sergeant William Albert Peacock
Sergeant Geoffrey Wilberforce Pearson
Flying Officer Arthur Peter Pease
Flying Officer George Charles Boyce Peters
Flight Sergeant Norman Taylor Phillips
Sergeant Leslie Pidd
Flying Officer Oswald St John Pigg
Squadron Leader Philip Campbell Pinkham AF
Flying Officer Richard Pryer Plummer
Pilot Officer Lawrence Lee Pyman

Pilot Officer John Basil Ramsay
Sergeant John William Ramshaw
Flying Officer Malcolm Ravenhill
Sergeant Leslie Arthur Edwin Reddington
Pilot Officer Hugh William Reilley
Flight Lieutenant Richard Carew Reynell
Pilot Officer Richard Arthur Rhodes
Flight Lieutenant William Henry Rhodes-Moorhouse
Flying Officer Alan Leslie Ricalton
Sergeant Marmaduke Ridley
Flight Lieutenant Reginald Frank Rimmer
Sergeant Robert Douglas Ritchie
Flying Officer Arthur Thomas Rose-Price
Flight Lieutenant Fredrick William Rushmer
Flying Officer Lionel Harold Schwind
Pilot Officer Kirkpatrick Maclure Sclanders
Sergeant Ernest Scott
Sergeant John Alan Scott
Flying Officer William John Moir Scott
Pilot Officer Lionel Argent Sears
Sergeant Martin Michael Shanahan
Flying Officer Ian Garstin Shaw
Pilot Officer Robert Henry Shaw
Sergeant Frederick Ernest Richard Shepherd
Pilot Officer Douglas Clayton Shepley
Sergeant Edmund Eric Shepperd
Flying Officer Lord Shuttleworth
Sergeant William Gerald Silver
Sergeant Frederick Albert Sibley
Sergeant Robert Black Sim
Flying Officer Geoffrey Mervyn Simpson
Sergeant Kenneth Barton Smith
Sergeant Arthur Dumbell Smith
Pilot Officer Denis Norman Evelyn Smith
Flying Officer Donald Sydney Smith
Pilot Officer Julian Langley Smither
Pilot Officer Neville David Solomon

Sergeant Mervyn Herbert Sprague
Sergeant Robert Edward Stevens
Squadron Leader Harold Morley Starr
Flying Officer Peter Cape Beauchamp St John
Flight Lieutenant George Edward Bowes Stoney
Sergeant Sidney George Stuckey
Pilot Officer John Alnod Peter Studd
Pilot Officer Norman Sutton
Flight Sergeant Charles Sydney
Flight Sergeant John Henry Tanner
Pilot Officer Alec Albert Grey Trueman
Flight Lieutenant Donald Eric Turner
Sergeant Frederick Fenton Vinyard
Sergeant John Victor Wadham
Pilot Officer Ernest Cecil John Wakeham
Sergeant Sidney Richard Ernest Wakeling
Acting Flight Lieutenant Stuart Crosby Walch
Sergeant Peter Kenneth Walley
Sergeant Rufus Arthur Ward
Acting Flight Lieutenant William Henry Cromwell Warner
Flying Officer Robin McGregor Waterston
Acting Flight Lieutenant Percy Stevenson Weaver
Pilot Officer Frank Kinneraly Webster
Flight Lieutenant John Terrance Webster
Flying Officer Kenneth Victor Wendel
Sergeant Thomas Emrys Westmoreland
Sergeant Basil Ewart Patrick Whall DFM
Pilot Officer Herbert Laurance Whitbread
Pilot Officer David Whitley
Flying Officer Edgar John Wilcox
Pilot Officer Timothy Seddon Wildblood
Sergeant Geoffrey Norman Wilkes
Squadron Leader Rodney Levett Wilkinson
Pilot Officer Robert Roy Wilson
Squadron Leader Cedric Watcyn Williams
Pilot Officer Desmond Gordon Williams
Flight Sergeant Eric Edward Williams

Pilot Officer Wycliff Stuart Williams
Pilot Officer Douglas Cyril Winter
Acting Flight Lieutenant Latham Carr Withall
Pilot Officer David Noel Woodger
Pilot Officer Charles Anthony Woods-Scawen DFC
Flying Officer Patrick Philip Woods-Scawen DFC
Flight Lieutenant Ronald Derek Gordon Wight DFC
Flight Lieutenant Herbert John Woodward DFC
Pilot Officer Kenneth Wilson Worsdell
Sergeant John Wright

Aircrew
Pilot Officer Allan Arthur Atkinson
Leading Aircraftman Albert Lawrence Austin
Aircraftman 2nd Class Charles Frederick Cooper
Sergeant John Gordon Bowley Fletcher
Sergeant Eric Cecil Gardiner
Sergeant Ronald Joseph Gouldstone
Aircraftman 2nd Class Arthur Jackson
Aircraftman 2nd Class Norman Jacobson
Pilot Officer Charles Edward Johnson
Sergeant Laurence Robert Karasek
Sergeant Francis John Keast
Pilot Officer Frederick Harry King DFM
Aircraftman 2nd Class John Patrick McCaul
Sergeant William Howard Machin
Aircraftman 2nd Class Reginald Irving Payne
Sergeant Harry Thomas Perry
Pilot Officer William Alan Pontin
Sergeant George Edward Shepperd
Sergeant Oswold Kenneth Sly
Sergeant Cyril Stephens
Sergeant Robert Charles Turner
Aircraftman 1st Class John Benjamin William Warren
Sergeant John Francis Wise
Sergeant Daniel Leslie Wright
Leading Aircraftman John Pile Wyatt

Royal Canadian Air Force
Pilots
Flying Officer Robert Leonard Edwards
Flying Officer O.J. Peterson
Flying Officer R. Smithers

Royal New Zealand Air Force
Air Crew
Sergeant David Ernest Hughes
Sergeant Lauritz Andrew Woodney Rasmussenn
Sergeant Robert Bett Mirk Young

Allied Foreign Personnel

(Working with Royal Air Force)

Belgian
Pilots
Pilot Officer Maurice Simon Henri Charles Buchin
Pilot Officer Georges Louis Joseph Doutrepont
Pilot Officer Alexis Rene Isidore Ghislain Jottard
Pilot Officer Jacques Arthur Laurent Philipeart
Pilot Officer A.E.A.D.J.G. Van Den Hove D'Ertsenryck

Czechoslovakian
Pilots
Sergeant J. Franciskek
Pilot Officer Emil Fechtner
Pilot Officer Vilem Goth
Sergeant Jaroslav Hlavac
Sergeant Veadimir Horsky
Sergeant Frantisek Marek
Pilot Officer Jaroslav Sterbacek

Polish
Pilots
Sergeant T. Andreszkow
Flying Officer J. Borowski

Sergeant M. Brzezowski
Flight Lieutenant J. Tadeusz Chlopik
Sergeant Stanislaw Duszynski
Flying Officer A. Gebrzynski
Pilot Officer Witold Glowacki
Sergeant Heliks Gmur
Acting Flying Officer Franciszek Gruszka
Flying Officer Wojciech Januszewicz
Flight Lieutenant F. Jasterebsky
Pilot Officer M.I.X. Krepski
Sergeant Josep Kwiecinski
Acting Flying Officer Kazimiers Lukaszewicz
Pilot Officer Janusz Macinski
Acting Flying Officer Antoni Ostowicz
Flying Officer L. Paszliewicz
Acting Flight Lieutenant Wilhelm Pankratz
Pilot Officer Stanislaw Pintkowski
Pilot Officer Mieczyslau Rozwadowski
Pilot Officer Michal Samolinski
Acting Flying Officer Michal Steborowski
Sergeant A. Suidak
Pilot Officer S. Wapnlarek
Sergeant Antoni Wojcicki
Sergeant S. Wojtowiczs
Sergeant J. Zaluski
Pilot Officer Pawel Zenker
Pilot Officer A. Zukowski

Those Attending the 20th Anniversary Reunion

Those recorded by the BBFA as planning to attend the Battle of Britain 20th anniversary reunion held at Bentley Priory on 15 September 1960. Names, ranks and post nominals are as listed by the BBFA at the time.

The Rt Hon Sir Winston Churchill KG OM CH MP did not attend but intended to send a message.

The Rt Hon The Lord Balfour of Inchyre MC
Air Chief Marshal The Lord Dowding GCB KCB CB GCVO CMG
Air Chief Marshal Sir Thomas Pike KCB CBE DFC Chief of the Air Staff
General Sir Frederick Pile GCB DSO MC LLD
Vice Admiral R.B. Davies VC CB DSO AFC RN Ret
Air Vice Marshal J.A. Boret CBE MC AFC
Group Captain A.B. Woodhall OBE

Members
Air Marshal Sir Hector McGregor KCB CBE DSO
Air Vice Marshal J. Grandy CB DSO
Air Vice Marshal S.F. Vincent CB DFC AFC
Air Commodore E.M. Donaldson CB CBE DSO AFC
Air Commodore H.A. Fenton CBE DSO DFC
Air Commodore G.F. Heycock DFC
Air Commodore P.G. Jameson CB DSO DFC
Air Commodore J.A. Leathart CB DSO
Air Commodore A.R.D. MacDonell DFC
Air Commodore E.J. Morris CBE DSO DFC
Air Commodore D.N. Roberts CBE AFC
Air Commodore F.E. Rosier CBE DSO
Air Commodore J.M. Thompson CBE DSO DFC AFC

Group Captain D.R.S. Bader CBE DSO DFC
Group Captain P.M. Brothers DSO DFC
Group Captain C.E.J. Baines CBE
Group Captain A.J. Banham
Group Captain H.A.C. Bird-Wilson DSO DFC AFC
Group Captain R. Berry DSO OBE DFC
Group Captain D. Crowley-Milling DSO DFC
Group Captain J. Cunningham DSO OBE DFC
Group Captain H.S. Darley DSO
Group Captain A.C. Deere DSO OBE DFC
Group Captain R.M.B. Duke-Woolley DSO DFC
Group Captain H.S.L. Dundas DSO DFC
Group Captain J. Ellis CBE DFC
Group Captain D.O. Finlay DFC AFC
Group Captain D.E. Gillam DSO DFC AFC
Group Captain T.P. Gleave CBE
Group Captain C.F. Gray DSO DFC
Group Captain J.H. Hill CBE
Group Captain A.P. Hope OBE DFC
Group Captain G.B. Johns DSO DFC AFC
Group Captain A.V.R. Johnstone DFC
Group Captain J.A. Kent DFC AFC
Group Captain J.E. McComb DFC
Group Captain A.G. Miller DFC
Group Captain R.V. Walker DSO
Group Captain J.W. White MBE
Group Captain E.W. Wooten DFC,AFC
Group Captain D.S. Wilson-Macdonald DSO DFC

Wing Commander H.R. Allen DFC
Wing Commander R.W. Arbon DFC
Wing Commander C.F. Babbage DFM
Wing Commander C.C.M. Baker OBE
Wing Commander P.P.C. Barthropp DFC AFC
Wing Commander E.G. Barwell DFC and bar
Wing Commander I.H. Bayles DFC

Wing Commander J.M Blazin DSO DFC
Wing Commander R.P. Beamont DSO OBE DFC
Wing Commander W. Blackadder DSO OBE
Wing Commander M.V. Blake DSO DFC
Wing Commander F.N. Brinsden
Wing Commander G.C. Brunner AFC
Wing Commander D.C. Bunch DSO DFC
Wing Commander E. Cassidy DFC AFC
Wing Commander D.L. Clackson MBE
Wing Commander I.H. Cosby DFC
Wing Commander D.G.S.R. Cox DFC
Wing Commander R.F.T. Doe DFC AFC
Wing Commander J. Fleming MBE
Wing Commander A.D. Forster DFC
Wing Commander J.R.H. Gayner DFC
Wing Commander A.L. Hamilton
Wing Commander N.P.W. Hancock,DFC
Wing Commander R.E. Havercroft AFC
Wing Commander B. Heath DFC
Wing Commander F.S. Hogg
Wing Commander B.J. Jennings AFC DFM
Wing Commander R.R. Mitchell MBE DFC
Wing Commander G.E. Morris
Wing Commander G.H. Nelson-Edwards DFC
Wing Commander P. Raymond DFC
Wing Commander G.L. Sinclair DFC
Wing Commander D.F.B. Sheen DFC and bar
Wing Commander F.M. Smith DFC
Wing Commander D.S. Wallen OBE
Wing Commander D.S. Wilson
Wing Commander H.M. Stephen DSO DFC
Wing Commander G.H. Westlake DSO DFC

Commander H.G.K. Bramah
Commander J.K. Quill OBE AFC

Squadron Leader D.L. Armitage DFC
Squadron Leader C.S. Bamberger DFC and bar
Squadron Leader M.P. Brown AFC
Squadron Leader K.M. Carver DFC
Squadron Leader L.H. Casson DFC AFC
Squadron Leader D.F. Chadwick
Squadron Leader G.G.A. Davies DFC
Squadron Leader R.F. Hamlyn AFC DFM
Squadron Leader S.V. Holloway OBE
Squadron Leader E.F. Leconte
Squadron Leader K.N.T. Lee DFC
Squadron Leader K.R. Lusty
Squadron Leader C.H. Macfie DFC
Squadron Leader A.G. McIntyre DFC
Squadron Leader M.J. Mansfield DSO DFC AFC
Squadron Leader E. Mayne AFC
Squadron Leader L.F. Ralls
Squadron Leader C.F. Rawnsley DSO DFC DFM
Squadron Leader S.N. Rose
Squadron Leader A.T. Sword-Daniels
Squadron Leader D.R. Turley-George DFC
Squadron Leader F. Usmar
Squadron Leader J. Whelan MBE AFC
Squadron Leader G.T. Williams OBE DFM
Squadron Leader V.C. Simmonds
Squadron Leader V.B.S. Verity

Flight Lieutenant H.A. Aitken
Flight Lieutenant J.H.B. Burgess
Flight Lieutenant D.G. Clift
Flight Lieutenant H. Cook
Flight Lieutenant J.H. Duart
Flight Lieutenant D. Fopp AFC
Flight Lieutenant D.H. Fox-Male
Flight Lieutenant R.M.D. Hall DFC
Flight Lieutenant N.D. Harding
Flight Lieutenant L.W. Harvey

Flight Lieutenant P.S. Hawke AFC
Flight Lieutenant P. Hillwood DFC
Flight Lieutenant D.H. Hone
Flight Lieutenant R.L. Jones
Flight Lieutenant R.A. Kings
Flight Lieutenant D.J. Looker
Flight Lieutenant J.W. McLaughlin
Flight Lieutenant M.H. Maggs DFC
Flight Lieutenant A.K. Malarowski
Flight Lieutenant J.G.P. Millard
Flight Lieutenant W.R. Moore
Flight Lieutenant Z. Olenski
Flight Lieutenant D.K. Parker
Flight Lieutenant F.S. Perkin
Flight Lieutenant R. Plenderleith
Flight Lieutenant L.A. Thorogood
Flight Lieutenant A.B. Tucker
Flight Lieutenant L.J. Tweed
Flight Lieutenant F.J. Twitchett
Flight Lieutenant J. Weber
Flight Lieutenant R. Wolton
Flight Lieutenant A.H. Deacon

Flying Officer A.W. Gear DFC
Flying Officer C.S. Lewis
Flying Officer K.A. Wilkinson

Warrant Officer P.H. Fox
Master Signaller W.M. Middlemiss DFC

Bibliography

Archives consulted include:
Battle of Britain Fighter Association archives, including those of Group Captain Tom Gleave and Wing Commander John Young. The research archive compiled by Bruce Burton.

Files consulted at the National Archives, Kew, including Air 2/6557, Air 16/672 and Air 20/4200. The Air Ministry Orders specified in the text. Various files held in the Library and Muniment Room at Westminster Abbey.

Amongst the publications consulted were:
Addison, Paul and Crang, Jeremy A, edited by. *The Burning Blue: a New History of the Battle of Britain*. Pimlico, 2000
Alexander, Kristen. *Australian Eagles*. Barrallier Books, Australia, 2013
Alexander, Kristen. *Australia's Few and the Battle of Britain*. NewSouth Books, Australia, 2014
Arnold, Keith. *Green Two, Sgt Dennis Noble*. Southern Counties Aviation Research/ Publications, 2003
Ashmore, Major General E.B. *Britain's Defence*. Longmans, Green & Co, 1929
Beaver, Paul. *Salute to The Few*. Newsdesk Communications, 2005
Bishop, Edward. *The Battle of Britain*. George Allen & Unwin, 1960
Bradley, D.L. *Locomotives of the Southern Railway, Part 2*. Railway Correspondence and Travel Society, 1976
Bungay, Stephen. *The Most Dangerous Enemy*. Aurum Press, 2000
Churchill, Winston S. *The Second World War, Vol ll, Their Finest Hour*. Cassell & Co, 1949
Colville, John. *The Fringes of Power*. Hodder and Stoughton, 1985
Cotter, Jarrod. *Battle of Britain Memorial Flight – 50 Years of Flying*. Pen & Sword Aviation, 2007
Crabb, Brian James. *Beyond the Call of Duty*. Shaun Tyas, 2006
Dean, Sir Maurice KCB KCMG. *The Royal Air Force and Two World Wars*, Littlehampton Books Services, 1979
Deere, Group Captain Alan C. DSO OBE DFC. *Nine Lives*. Coronet Books edition, 1961
Embry, Air Chief Marshal Sir Basil. *Mission Completed*. Methuen, 1957
Flint, Peter. *Dowding and Headquarters Fighter Command*. Airlife Publishing, 1996
Foxley-Norris, Christopher. *A Lighter Shade of Blue*. Ian Allan, 1978

Gleed, Wing Commander Ian DFC. *Arise to Conquer*. Random House, 1942
Hunting, Penelope (edited by). *The Hunting History*, Hunting plc, 1991
Ingram, Bruce (edited by). *Winston Churchill: The Greatest Figure of our Time. Illustrated London News*, 1954
Jenkins, Roy, *Churchill*. Macmillan, 2001
Jenkyns, Richard. *Westminster Abbey*. Profile Books, 2011 edition
Joubert, Air Chief Marshal Sir Philip. *The Third Service*. Thames & Hudson, 1955
Linlithgow, Marquess of. *Wings of Destiny*, Macmillan & Co, 1943
MacDonell Donald, edited by MacDonell, Lois and Mackay, Anne. *From Dogfight to Diplomacy*. Pen & Sword, 2005
Mason, Peter D. *Nicolson VC*, Geerings of Ashford, 1991
Montague-Smith, Patrick. *Debrett's Correct Form*. Futura Publications, 1979 edition
Ogley, Bob. *Biggin on the Bump*. Froglets Publications, 1990
Orange, Vincent. *Churchill and his Airmen*. Grub Street, 2013
Orange, Vincent. *Dowding of Fighter Command*. Grub Street Publishing, 2008
Orange, Vincent. *Sir Keith Park*. Methuen, 1984
Page, Geoffrey. *Shot Down in Flames*. Grub Street, 1999
Probert, Air Commodore Henry and Cox, Sebastian. *The Battle Re-thought*. RAF Historical Society, 1991
Ramsey, Winston G., edited by. *The Battle of Britain Then and Now*. Battle of Britain Prints International, 1980
Ray, John. *The Battle of Britain New Perspectives*. Arms and Armour Press, 1994
Sansom, William. *Westminster in War*. Faber and Faber, 1947
Saunders, Andy. *Finding The Few*. Grub Street, 2009
Terraine, John. *The Right of The Line*. Hodder and Stoughton, 1985
Vincent, Air Vice Marshal S.F. *Flying Fever*. Jarrolds, 1972
Wallace, Graham. *RAF Biggin Hill*. Putnam & Co, 1969
Wilkinson, James. *Henry VII's Lady Chapel*. Tudsbury Press, 2013 edition
Wood, Derek and Dempster, Derek, *The Narrow Margin*, Pen & Sword Military Classics edition, 2003
Wright, Robert. *Dowding and the Battle of Britain*. Military Book Society edition, 1969
Wykeham, Air Vice Marshal P.G. *Fighter Command*, Putnam, 1960
Wynn, Kenneth G. *A Clasp for The Few*. Author, 1981
Wynn, Kenneth G. *Men of the Battle of Britain*. Third edition, Frontline with Battle of Britain Memorial Trust, 2015 (manuscript of)
Ziegler, Philip. *London at War 1939–45*. Sinclair-Stevenson, 1939–1945
Air Chief Marshal Dowding's despatch, The Battle of Britain, August 1941 and supplement to the *London Gazette*, 10 September 1946
Anonymous. *St George's Royal Air Force Chapel of Remembrance*, Biggin, Hill, Kent. Friends of Biggin Hill Chapel, 2007
Anonymous. *The Battle of Britain*. HMSO, 1941

Daily Telegraph, The Times, Daily Express, The Guardian (previously *Manchester Guardian*), *News Chronicle, Hansard, Illustrated London News, Grimsby Telegraph, Flight, War & Society, The Spectator, Britain at War, After the Battle, 1940, The Aeroplane, Who Was Who, The Studio, Express & Star, Black Country Bugle, Pontefract & Castleford Express.* Various annual Battle of Britain brochures issued by RAFA.

www.battleofbritainmemorial.org
www.bbm.org.uk
www.bentleypriory.org
www.bucksas.org.uk
www.nationaltrust.org
www.newulsterbiography.co.uk
www.oxforddnb.com
www.raf.mod.uk
www.rafweb.org
www.rocassoc.org.uk
www.shoreham-aircraft-museum.co.uk
www.westminster-abbey.org

The Author

Geoff Simpson was born in Kent and grew up in south-east London in the years after the Second World War. He has worked in journalism and public relations and is now a freelance journalist. He has studied the Battle of Britain for many years and has written extensively on the subject. Geoff is a Trustee of the Battle of Britain Memorial Trust, a member of the RAF Historical Society and an Honorary Member of the Pen and Sword Club.

Geoff is married with two adult children and lives in Hazel Grove near Stockport.

Index